CONSTRUCTION,

MANAGEMENT

AND

INVESTMENT POTENTIAL

OF

MOBILE HOME

AND

RECREATIONAL VEHICLE

PARKS

By

Robert H. Nulsen

LIBRARY OF CONGRESS CARD NUMBER   77-116495

STANDARD BOOK NUMBER 87593-095-6

XRε 9-16-70

PUBLISHED BY

Trail-R-Club of America

America's Largest Publisher of Books
Pertaining to Recreational Vehicles
and Mobile Home Living

Box 1376   Beverly Hills, California 90213

PRINTED IN THE UNITED STATES OF AMERICA

OTHER BOOKS BY
ROBERT H. NULSEN

Mobile Home Manual (two volumes)

All About Parks For Mobile Homes and Trailers

Tips For Trailer Traveling — Tips for Trailer Towing

Mobile Home Heaters and Air-conditioners

How to Buy Mobile Homes, Travel Trailers, and Campers

Travel Trailer, Vacation Trailer Manual

Mr. Nulsen has also edited over 40 other books in the mobile home and recreational field including two books relating to the park industry by Mr. Fred Sparer:

How to Build Mobile Home Parks

How to Build Recreational Vehicle Parks

TABLE OF CONTENTS

Introduction 5

The Industry 9

Success Factors 112

Steps To A Profitable Park Investment 119

Income Potential 126

Site Location 140

Design and Engineering 147

Construction 196

Financing 199

Park Management 203

Appendix 217

INTRODUCTION

In the past few years there has been a tremendous surge in interest in the development of both recreational vehicle and mobile home parks. The interest comes from individual land owners who have property they are interested in developing and managing for themselves; it comes from the conventional home builder who is taking a hard look at the mobile home and recreational vehicle industry as a field in which he may use his construction facilities and capabilities, and it comes from investors of all types who believe that these two exploding industries offer an opportunity for worthwhile investments. Such investors are both individuals and corporations.

Speaking from personal experience and personal knowledge, I feel that such interest is justified: both the mobile home and recreational vehicle park industry do offer the potential for an excellent return on invested capital. The explosive rate of growth in mobile home and recreational vehicle sales combined with the long period of time between planning a park and filling it means that for some time to come there will be a scarcity of spaces in the United States, both for mobile homes and recreational vehicles. This critical shortage is one factor which leads to a high return for the investor.

A problem encountered by those who are investigating the industry is the lack of published material designed to give them a quick overview of the industry without going into distracting detail. This book is designed to meet this need. Because our purpose in this publication is to give the reader a quick summary of the industry, a summary which will enable him to determine whether or not he wishes to dig deeper, our approach will be to remain as non-technical as possible.

For those who want to investigate the industry in depth, there is a considerable amount of published material. For example, the Trail-R-Club of America, publisher of this book, has two technical publications available on the subject of park construction. One, *How to Build Mobile Home Parks,* and another, *How to Build Recreational Vehicle Parks,* are both authored by Mr. Fred Sparer and edited by the author of this book. Both of these are highly technical publications. The Trail-R-Club of America also publishes a large number of books dealing with both the mobile home and recreational vehicle industry; these are available to those who want to know more about specific aspects of the industry.

One aspect of this industry that requires in-depth study for successful park operation is the field of management. The only thing in print at the present time on this complex subject is a home study course published by Park Management Associates, Box 1417, Beverly Hills, California 90213. I am currently working with another author who is preparing a comprehensive book on the subject of both mobile home and recreational vehicle park management. It would appear, however, that the completion of this publication, due to the magnitude of the project, is at this time at least 18 to 24 months away. We will deal tangentially with management in this book, however.

There are very competent technical experts in this industry available to those who want to proceed further. There are architects who have had considerable experience in designing and building parks; there are contractors who have had similar experience; there are firms proficient in the field of management who work under property management contracts or for consulting fees. Sometimes it is difficult for the uninitiated to locate such experts. The most reliable way to get in touch with industry experts is to contact any of our industry's major trade associations. There are four large national associations.

Mobile Housing Association of America
39 S. LaSalle St.
Chicago, Illinois 60603

Mobile Homes Manufacturers Association
20 N. Wacker Drive
Chicago, Illinois 60606

Recreational Vehicle Institute
2720 Des Plaines Ave.
Des Plaines, Illinois 60018

Trailer Coach Association
1340 W. Third St.
Los Angeles, California 90017

In addition to these associations there are many local and regional associations who can put you in touch with local technical experts. The names and addresses of local associations can be obtained by writing to any of the national associations.

The use of technical assistance for those who want to enter the park industry is strongly recommended. Although the fees paid by such individuals or firms may appear high at first, it is inevitable that in the long run the retention of such advisors will considerably reduce overall costs for any project undertaken. A park development is an extremely complex undertaking requiring many components for success.

The novice, unguided by an expert, is almost certain to make many mistakes which, in the end, can be most costly; these mistakes can actually lead to the failure of the development. Many types of technical advice are available. Through technically oriented personnel you can obtain appraisals of mobile home or recreational vehicle properties, cost estimates on new developments, assistance in obtaining zoning, assistance in obtaining financing, site planning, engineering, and management help.

A large number of both mobile home and recreational vehicle parks have been built in the past by private individuals who purchased land and did their own contracting. This is still possible, but the project is simplified and made less costly if professional advice is sought. Such individuals usually kept their development to the 25 to 75 space size, and in many cases did much of the construction work themselves. The park industry in the last few years, however, has really come of age. The small developments are now the minority. Most of our modern developments are very sophisticated, large developments. The size of the acreage, the size of the plant, the sophistication of development, and sophistication in management have all brought the large mobile home park and recreational vehicle park to a very profitable level.

THE INDUSTRY

We speak of the mobile home and recreational vehicle industry as a single industry. Putting them into one package is probably a result of historical factors. The mobile home is an outgrowth of the early trailers that were manufactured basically for recreational purposes. They were later adapted for permanent living accommodations. Even today, the same factory often manufactures both mobile homes and recreational vehicles. The two are really *two* entirely separate industries, however. They serve two separate markets: mobile homes serve the housing market and recreational vehicles serve the leisure market. There is some overlapping, of course. The retired couple living and traveling in a large travel trailer or motor home is a case in point.

Both the mobile home and recreational vehicle markets are literally exploding as this publication is prepared. We shall provide you with statistics to acquaint you with the facts. Not only are they presently exploding, but they both appear to have fabulous futures. The recreational vehicle's future seems assured because of the high and increasing income level of the American public combined with more leisure time. The mobile home industry's future seems most bright because it appears to be the wave of the future for fulfilling the needs of the housing market. Conventional housing seems to have priced itself out of the low-price, and even middle price, market; the mobile home is filling this gap admirably.

It would seem inadvisable to start a discussion of the mobile home and recreational vehicle park industry without a brief description of the product that is placed in the park. We will now discuss briefly the mobile home and the recreational vehicle.

Mobile Home

The American concept of a trailer built for travel appeared in the early 1920's. During the depression years, some lived in their trailers rather than in homes for reasons of pure economy. The accommodations were crude. Soon permanent dwellers began devising ways and means of improving their living conditions. When World War II came along, the United States Government gave the industry a real impetus by purchasing thousands of trailers (size 8' by 20') for use as wartime housing. Many who were forced into such accommodations found that they enjoyed this type of living; this generated efforts to improve the quality of the product. The 1950's saw tremendous changes in the trailers — so many, in fact, that it became necessary to distinguish between TRAILERS (used for traveling) and MOBILE HOMES (used as permanent residences).

The accepted industry definition today for a mobile home is as follows:

> A mobile home is a movable, or portable dwelling constructed to be towed on its own chassis, connected to utilities, and designed with a permanent foundation for year-round living. It consists of one or more units that can be folded, collapsed, or telescoped when towed and expanded later for additional cubic capacity, or of two or more units, separately towable but designed to be joined into one intregal unit, capable of being again separated into components for repeated towing.

New mobile homes are sold fully equipped, including major appliances, furniture, draperies, lamps, and carpeting. Optional equipment includes such items as air-conditioning, automatic dishwashers, automatic garbage disposals, radios, TVs, and any other appliance found in the modern, American home. The mobile home is centrally heated by gas, oil, or electricity. The purchaser has many choices of decor, such as Early American, French Provincial, Oriental, Mediterranean, Traditional, or Contemporary. Mobile homes are designed with a spacious living room, dining room, kitchen or kitchen dinette, one or two bathrooms, and one, two, or more bedrooms with built-in custom cabinetry and closets.

An average size mobile home would be approximately 12' x 60', with a retail selling price of approximately $6000. Prices in the industry, however, vary from $4000 to $15,000, depending upon quality. Furnished mobile homes sell for approximately $9 per square foot compared in price to an unfurnished site-built house at about $20 per square foot. Larger mobile homes (double wides or expandables) provide from 1000 to 1500 square feet and retail at prices of approximately $8000 to $15,000 and up. By contrast, the median price of a 1200 square foot conventional home (less furnishings) would be $22,000 to $26,000. In 1968 mobile homes represented 96 percent of all single family homes sold under $12,500; 90 percent of all single family homes sold under $15,000; and nearly 60 percent of the 503,000 single family homes sold at any price. On the pages which follow we have included pictures of various size mobile homes to acquaint the reader with the types of units currently being marketed.

Courtesy: Hi-Rise Mobile Homes
A two story mobile house? Indeed it is . . . and it is mobile.

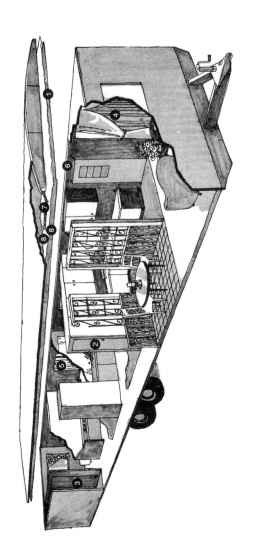

Courtesy: Kirkwood Mobile Homes

Courtesy: Trailer Coach Association

Street scene of a deluxe mobile home park in Southern California.

Courtesy: Champion Home Builders Co.
A double wide mobile home set on site by Champion Home Builders Co.

Courtesy: Guernsey City
Viewing deluxe mobile home park in Tampa, Florida.

Courtesy: Budger Homes Division of Wick Building Systems, Inc.
A double wide mobile home.

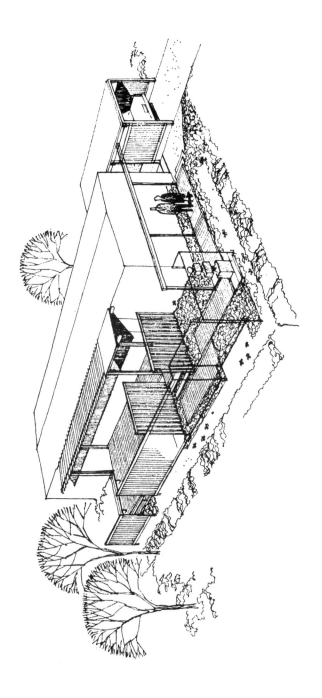

Courtesy: M & R Housing Merchandiser

Lot plan and lot view of King City Estates park in Tigard, Oregon.

THE INDUSTRY

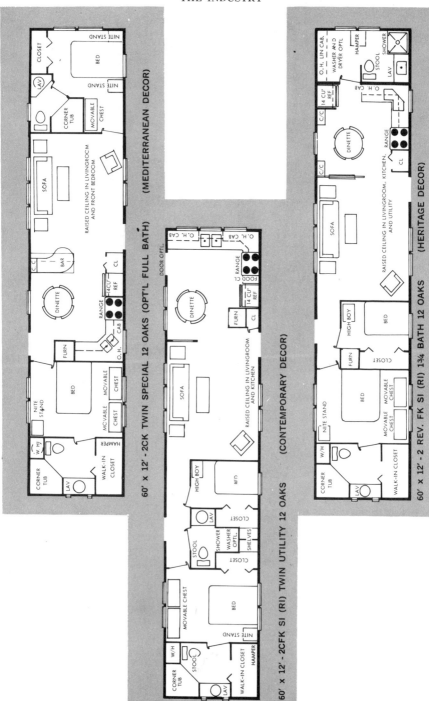

60' x 12' - 2CK TWIN SPECIAL 12 OAKS (OPT'L FULL BATH) (MEDITERRANEAN DECOR)

60' x 12' - 2CFK SI (RI) TWIN UTILITY 12 OAKS (CONTEMPORARY DECOR)

60' x 12' - 2 REV. FK SI (RI) 1¾ BATH 12 OAKS (HERITAGE DECOR)

Typical floor plans of a popular selling size.

Courtesy: Delta Homes Corp.

60' x 12' - 2 RAISED FK SI (RI) 12 OAKS (OLD ENGLISH DECOR)

64' x 12' - 2 FLACK FL SI (RI) 12 OAKS (MEDITERRANEAN DECOR)

19

Jack Kneass Photo

A single wide Universal mobile home with add on features set in a Southern California Park.

55' x 20' — 2 BEDROOM — 2 BATH MODEL 440 BUDGER TWENTY WIDE

55' x 20' — 3 BEDROOM — 2 BATH MODEL 441 BUDGER TWENTY WIDE

Courtesy: Budger Mfg. Co.

Typical floor plans of popular size double wide mobile homes.

Courtesy: Budger Mfg. Co.

Bedroom and living room in a Budger double wide mobile home.

Courtesy: Budger Mfg. Co.

Entrance and kitchen of a 24' x 60' Budger double wide mobile home.

1   SCHULT roofs have high density fibre glass insulation and sufficient area for ventilation to disperse any inner roof condensation. Numerous roof vents are installed to facilitate roof air ventilation.

2   3   SCHULT specially designed galvanized steel roofs overlap the side wall exterior metal insuring that no leaks will occur. SCHULT installs a positive non-hardening ribbon caulking line under and over the roof lap and under the drip rail.

4   SCHULT applies a roof sheathing between the metal roof and roof beams to act as a blotter in the event of any roof condensation.

5   6   SCHULT installs heavy duty density fibre glass insulation over a 30-30-30 vapor seal that prohibits interior vapor entry into the roof cavity.

7   SCHULT manufactures its own roof beams, using a continuous chord truss with quarter inch plywood gussets glued to both sides of the beam. All beams are on 16" centers.

8   SCHULT uses either high grade decorative acoustical or genuine plywood paneling for interior ceilings as the decor dictates.

9   SCHULT unitized structure ties the sidewall to the floor with a continuous ⅝"x8" bottom plate and the roof to the top of the sidewall with a continuous 1"x6" top plate. These plates are all glued to the studs. This assures that all body members and under structure, floors, sides, ends and roof and very essentially, the glueing of the interior plywood to the stud, absorb all the strain to which a mobile home is subjected. The old-style conventional construction is completely eliminated (there is no reliance on tin banding strips—thin metal plate gussets as is conventional).

10   SCHULT sidewalls are a nominal 3" thickness. Vertical studs are dadoed and securely fastened to become a part of the unitized structure.

11   The SCHULT Silent Comfort Control Heating System with its cold air returns maintains comfort from floor to ceiling, under outside temperatures to 40 degrees below zero! The SCHULT Silent Heat System permits noiseless operation, has complete under-floor return air distribution thus affording warm floors and plumbing protection.

12   SCHULT assures that the one piece oversized heat ducts—positively sealed—are installed between the floor and sub-floor.

13   SCHULT floors have continuous longitudinal floor joists with supporting cross stringers on 12" centers and provides a minimum of 10 inches of unsupported floor space.

14   In Schult 60' and larger models, walls are doubly insulated with high density fibre glass batts between studs and a continuous sheet of perforated reinforced aluminum foil. The fibre glass batts and perforated reinforced aluminum foil completely covers the entire side wall framing behind the aluminum exterior side walls. This method insures against air leaks, inner wall condensation and heat loss. The "R" factor substantially exceeds M.H.M.A. or A.S.A. requirements.

15   SCHULT floors have high density fibre glass insulation over weatherproof

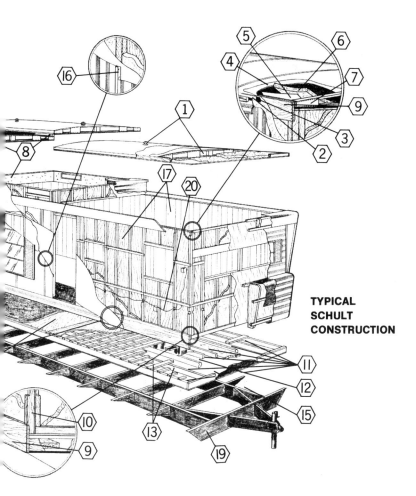

**TYPICAL
SCHULT
CONSTRUCTION**

barriers of asphalt impregnated insulation board.

16   SCHULT aluminum exterior wall construction is constructed with lock seams at the upper horizontal trim line and all critical vertical and horizontal side wall aluminum joints are at the insert sections.

17   All interior walls are of quarter inch genuine natural plywoods enhanced by modern high gloss finish. These panels are firmly glued and securely fastened to the side wall studding.

18   SCHULT base flooring is of ⅝ ″ underlayment with a surface of either vinyl floor covering or carpet.

19   SCHULT provides all steel—welded frames that are secured to the unitized body—not only at every outrigger—but at all cross members—plus the front and rear ends—to make the frame an integral part of the unitized structure. This frame is designed for 50% overload at all points of impact.

20   SCHULT has heavy duty 3 wire house type wiring with grounded circuits and provides 220 V circuits.

Courtesy: Schult Homes

Mobile homes are built to rigid standards. In many states the enforcing of standards is a state agency function.

25

Courtesy: Champion Home Builders Co.

This photo and the ones on the two following pages show factory procedures and quality built into mobile homes.

Courtesy: Nashua Homes

Kitchen of a Nashua mobile home.

Two living room views in modern double wide mobile homes.

Courtesy: Marlette Homes

Two photos of Marlette mobile home interiors.

Courtesy: Guerdon Industries, Inc.
Modular housing, a product of the mobile home industry is predicted to be a major factor in the housing industry of the future.

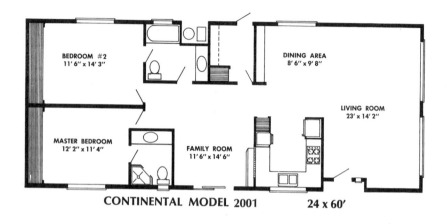

CONTINENTAL MODEL 2001   24 x 60'

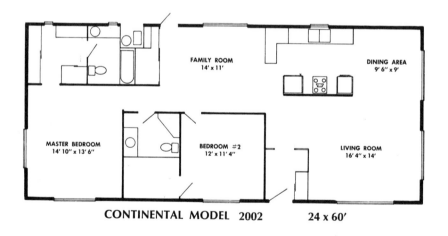

CONTINENTAL MODEL 2002   24 x 60'

Courtesy: Cambridge Mobile Homes
Typical floor plans for 24' x 60' double wides (1200 square feet of living space).

Mobile Home Industry Growth

To acquaint you with the growth of the industry we reproduce now statistical information describing the growth of the industry.

MOBILE HOMES SHIPMENTS

Year	Manufacturers' Shipments to Dealers in U.S.	Retail Sales (Estimated)
1968	317,950	$1,907,700,000
1967	240,360	1,370,052,000
1966	217,300	1,238,610,000
1965	216,470	1,212,232,000
1964	191,320	1,071,392,000
1963	150,840	862,064,000
1962	118,000	661,000,000
1961	90,200	505,000,000
1960	103,700	518,000,000
1959	120,500	602,000,000
1958	102,000	510,000,000
1957	119,300	596,000,000
1956	124,330	622,000,000
1955	111,900	462,000,000
1954	76,000	325,000,000
1953	76,900	322,000,000
1952	83,000	320,000,000
1951	67,300	248,000,000
1950	63,100	216,000,000
1949	46,200	122,000,000
1948	85,500	204,000,000
1947	60,000	146,000,000

Prior to 1947, production varied from 1,300 in 1930 upward to 60,000 in 1947.
10-wide homes came into mass production in 1955.
12-wide homes came into mass production in 1962.

Courtesy: Mobile Homes Manufacturers Association

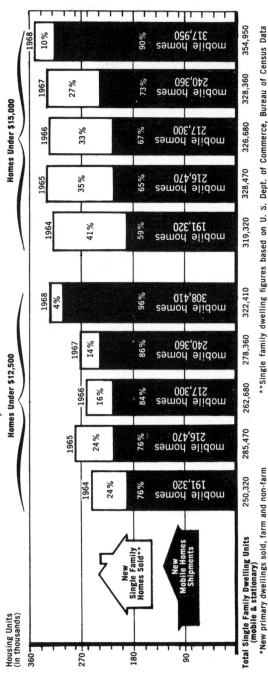

MOBILE HOMES and TOTAL SINGLE FAMILY DWELLING SALES*

In 1968 mobile homes represented 96% of all single family homes sold under $12,500; 90% of all single family homes sold under $15,000; and they were nearly equal to 60% of the 530,000 single family homes sold at any price.**

Housing Units (in thousands)

Homes Under $15,000

Year	mobile homes	% mobile	% single family
1968	317,950	90%	10%
1967	240,360	73%	27%
1966	217,300	67%	33%
1965	216,470	65%	35%
1964	191,320	59%	41%

Homes Under $12,500

Year	mobile homes	% mobile	% single family
1968	308,410	96%	4%
1967	240,360	86%	14%
1966	217,300	84%	16%
1965	216,470	76%	24%
1964	191,320	76%	24%

New Single Family Homes Sold**

New Mobile Homes Shipments

Total Single Family Dwelling Units (mobile & stationary)

	1964	1965	1966	1967	1968
	250,320	285,470	262,680	278,360	322,410
	319,320	328,470	326,680	328,360	354,950

*New primary dwellings sold, farm and non-farm

**Single family dwelling figures based on U. S. Dept. of Commerce, Bureau of Census Data

Courtesy: Mobile Homes Manufacturers Association

MOBILE HOME FAMILIES*

More than 5 million people live in mobile homes. The median mobile home family has 2.49 persons.

Persons in Household	Mobile Home Survey†	1967 CPS** All Families†
1	10.7%	15.5%
2	39.7	28.3
3	23.9	17.6
4	14.5	16.1
5	7.0	10.6
6	2.8	5.9
7	1.4	6.0
Median Persons	2.49	2.85

Household Composition		
2 or more Persons	89.6%	84.5%
Husband-Wife	84.6	72.2
Other Male Head	1.3	2.7
Female Head	3.6	9.6
1 Person	10.7	15.5

Age Groups		
Less than 35 years	49.4%	23.6%
35 to 54	29.4	40.4
55 to 64	11.8	16.7
65 and over	9.3	19.4

Children's Age	Mobile Home Survey* 2 or more Persons Household Head†	1967 CPS** All Families†
None under 18	46.9%	44.0%
1 Child under 18	26.0	17.8
2 or more under 18	27.1	38.2
None under 6	62.8	71.6
1 or more under 6	37.2	28.4

Income		
$ 4,999 and under	27.6%	28.2%
5,000 to 6,999	27.2	17.8
7,000 to 9,999	29.4	24.4
10,000 to 14,999	13.2	20.4
15,000 or more	2.5	9.2
Median Dollars	$6,620	$7,440

Education		
Less than 8th grade	7.5%	13.2%
8th through 12th grade	74.5	64.4
1 year or more college	18.0	22.4
Median School Years	11.6	12.1

Occupations		
Professional, Technical	7.1%	10.9%
Managers, Officers, Proprietors	8.1	15.0
Craftsmen (skilled)	21.5	16.5
Operatives (semi-skilled)	21.4	15.7
Clerical, Sales	7.2	10.5
Service	4.8	6.2
Laborers (non-farm)	7.5	3.7
Farm Laborers	1.4	1.0
Not Employed, or Active Military Duty, or not in Labor Force	20.9	20.5

*Based on a survey of home owners conducted by Bureau of Census for Department of Housing & Urban Development of 2,900 mobile homes purchased from 10/1/65 through 9/30/66 and used as primary residences.

**Current Population Survey.

†Totals may not add due to rounding.

Since World War II, 2,926,980 mobile homes have been produced. Approximately 70% of these are currently in use as primary year-round dwellings, of which 50% are in mobile home communities.

Courtesy: Mobile Homes Manufacturers Association

Of vital interest to the park developer is the question of what size lots he should provide. This, of course, relates to the size mobile homes which are selling in his community, and what technological developments will take place in the future which might affect the size of mobile homes. Below we quote statistics on a U.S. industry-wide basis showing the size of mobile homes shipped in the United States in 1967 compared to 1968.

Width	Average Length	% of Total Shipments 1967	1968
8'	29' to 45'	.3%	.1%
10'	45' to 60'	7.3	2.2
12'	54' to 65'	84.1	85.9
Sectional homes (Double wides)	40' to 65'	6.3	8.2
Expandables	50' to 65'	2.0	3.6
		100.0%	100.0%

The above figures demonstrate that there is a tendency for the units to increase in size. This trend has been continuing for years. The park developer, of course, must be concerned with what size units are selling in the area in which he is planning to develop a park. Statistical data of this nature is fortunately available. It is published quarterly in *Mobile Homes Trailer Dealer* magazine, a trade journal for the industry, whose offices are at 6299 Northwest Highway, Chicago, Illinois 60631. The publisher of this magazine also publishes an annual Market Survey or study which details shipments on a regional basis for any particular year. The product mix is clearly defined and is of immense value in assisting a developer in determining lot sizes.

None of the statistics refer to 14' wide mobile homes; up until recently, they have been a curiosity. There are now 12 states permitting 14' wides, and there is the possibility that this trend may spread across the nation. Special arrangements, of course, must be made for moving units of this width. An interesting article on the future of the 14' wide appeared in the October 1969 issue of *Mobile and Recreational Housing Merchandiser* magazine. This trade publication is published by the Vance Publishing Corporation, located at 300 West Adams Street, Chicago, Illinois 60606, and it, like *Mobile Home Travel Trailer Dealer Magazine*, regularly contains a wealth of industry statistics that are of value to the park developer. We have printed on the next page a map taken from the *Mobile and Recreational Housing Merchandiser* depicting a prediction concerning the spread of the 14' wide movement.

The Recreational Vehicle

Let us now turn our attention to the recreational vehicle. They may, in general, be classified into four main categories, although there are a few maverick products which defy catergorization. The automobile with a folding tent which erects on top of the car, or the station wagon into various camping equipment is fitted on such occasions as may be desired, are examples of mavericks that defy classification. The four basic categories are: (1) tent camping trailers; 2) truck campers; (3) travel trailers; and (4) motor homes.

Tent Camping Trailers

Tent camping trailers are structures mounted on wheels and have collapsible side walls of fabric, plastic, or other types of pliable material. These compact units fold out into large, tent-like structures which will sleep two to eight people. Some models feature cooking facilities, chemical toilets, large awnings, and attachable screened extra rooms. They are easily towed by the modern automobile and are relatively inexpensive, selling for as little as $300. They do run as high as several thousands dollars for luxury units. The average price would be in the vicinity of $800. The tent camping trailer's share of the recreational vehicle market in 1968 was 23.76 percent.

Truck Campers

Truck campers are portable structures designed to be loaded onto or fixed to the bed or chassis of a truck. Such recreational vehicles do not require special license in most states. They are popular among sportsmen because of their rugged capabilities which permit travel into remote areas. Smaller units simply slide onto the bed of a one-half-ton

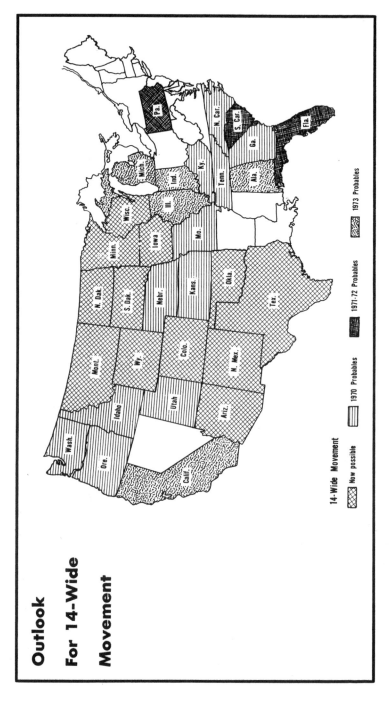

Outlook
For 14-Wide
Movement

14-Wide Movement

Now possible | 1970 Probables | 1971-72 Probables | 1973 Probables

Courtesy: M & R Housing Merchandiser

The following data is reprinted through the courtesy of Mobile Home/Recreational Vehicle Dealer Magazine. Figures show shipments to dealers for the second quarter of 1969.

SOUTH ATLANTIC	% INCREASE / % DECREASE	PRODUCT MIX			MOST POPULAR MODELS	
Delaware 560 MH shipped	− 1.78%	10wide — .42%	12wide — 95.77%	Doublewides — 3.81%	1. 60-64' 12wide 2. 50-54' 12wide 3. Doublewides 12wide	62.3% 21.0% 3.3%
Washington, D. C. 280 MH shipped	+428.30%	12wide — 100%			1. 60-64' 12wides 2. 50-54' 12wide 3. 40-44' 12wide	59.3% 36.0% 4.0%
Florida 7186 MH shipped	+ 36.30%	10wide — .39%	12wide — 90.41%	Doublewides — 5.44% Expandables — 2.47% Miscellaneous — 1.29%	1. 60-64' 12wide 2. 50-54' 12wide 3. 40-44' 12wide	52.5% 24.2% 8.7%
Georgia 5833 MH shipped	+45.97%	10wide — 1.06%	12wide — 96.54%	Doublewides — 1.18% Expandables — 1.06% Miscellaneous — .16%	1. 60-64' 12wide 2. 50-54' 12wide 3. 40-44' 12wide	54.06% 19.42% 14.80%
Maryland 751 MH shipped	+ 17.16%	10wide — 1.27%	12wide — 94.60%	Doublewides — .95% Expandables — 3.18%	1. 60-64' 12wide 2. 50-54' 12wide 3. Expandables & 65-69'	66.98% 19.36% 3.18%
North Carolina 6719 MH shipped	+ 29.68%	10wide — 1.06%	12wide — 96.88%	Doublewides — 1.10% Expandables — .14% Miscellaneous — .82%	1. 60-64' 12wide 2. 50-54' 12wide 3. 40-44' 12wide	51.12% 19.77% 15.94%
South Carolina 3341 MH shipped	+ 35.37%	10wide — .64%	12wide — 97.51%	Doublewides — .93% Expandables — .28% Miscellaneous — .64%	1. 60-64' 12wide 2. 50-54' 12wide 3. 40-44' 12wide	52.53% 22.63% 11.80%
Virginia 2929 MH shipped	+ 48.30%	10wide — .33%	12wide — 98.12%	Doublewides — 1.31% Expandables — .24%	1. 60-64' 12wide 2. 50-54' 12wide 3. 40-44' 12wide	59.13% 23.59% 7.37%
West Virginia 1221 MH shipped	+ 55.54%	10wide — 2.54%	12wide — 92.18%	Doublewides — 2.74% Expandables — 2.54%	1. 60-64' 12wide 2. 50-54' 12wide 3. 40-44' 12wide	61.84% 21.72% 3.13%
TOTAL MH shipped — 28,820		% of Total Projection — 25.5%				

CANADA	% INCREASE % DECREASE	PRODUCT MIX		MOST POPULAR MODELS	
Canada 1808 MH shipped	+159.77%	10wide — .79% 12wide — 96.58%	Doublewide — 2.37% Expandable — .26%	1. 60-64' 12wide 2. 50-54' 12wide 3. 40-44' 12wide	42.42% 28.72% 18.05%

TOTAL MH shipped — 1808

% of Total Projection — 1.60%

EAST NORTH CENTRAL	% INCREASE % DECREASE	PRODUCT MIX		MOST POPULAR MODELS	
Illinois 2844 MH shipped	+28.34%	8wide — .08% 10wide — 1.34% 12wide — 88.04%	Doublewides — 5.94% Expandables — 4.52% Miscellaneous — .08%	1. 60-64' 12wide 2. 50-54' 12wide 3. Expandables	60.87% 19.82% 4.52%
Indiana 2943 MH shipped	+36.44%	8wide — .24% 10wide — .16% 12wide — 91.24%	Doublewides — 4.71% Expandables — 3.57% Miscellaneous — .08%	1. 60-64' 12wide 2. 50-54' 12wide 3. Expandables	59.53% 22.46% 3.57%
Michigan 5639 MH shipped	+38.86%	8wide — .42% 10wide — .30% 12wide — 84.42%	Expandables — 10.46% Expandables — 4.15% Miscellaneous — .25%	1. 60-64' 12wide 2. 50-54' 12wide 3. Doublewides 12wide	59.21% 17.28% 6.69%
Ohio 4322 MH shipped	+35.78%	8wide — .39% 10wide — .27% 12wide — 87.10%	Doublewides — 6.01% Expandables — 6.23%	1. 60-64' 12wide 2. 50-54' 12wide 3. Expandables	63.84% 14.44% 6.23%
Wisconsin 1872 MH shipped	+41.60%	8wide — .51% 10wide — .51% 12wide — 80.54% 14wide — 5.89%	Doublewides — 6.53% Expandables — 1.15% Miscellaneous — 4.87%	1. 60-64' 12wide 2. 50-54' 12wide 3. 40-44' 12wide	50.06% 14.98% 9.60%

TOTAL MH shipped — 17,620

% of Total Projection — 15.59%

ALASKA	% INCREASE % DECREASE	PRODUCT MIX		MOST POPULAR MODELS	
Alaska 353 MH shipped	+ 14.61%	8wide — 2.03% 12wide — 83.11%	Doublewides — 9.46% Expandables — 5.40%	1. 60-64' 12wide 2. 40-44' 12wide 3. Doublewides 12wide	60.81% 8.78% 8.78%
TOTAL MH shipped — 353			% of Total Projection — .31%		

NEW ENGLAND	% INCREASE % DECREASE	PRODUCT MIX		MOST POPULAR MODELS	
Connecticut 535 MH shipped	+ 40.05%	12wide — 80.97%	Doublewides — 13.72% Expandables — 2.21% Miscellaneous — 3.10%	1. 60-64' 12wide 2. 50-54' 12wide 3. Doublewides 12wide	53.98% 19.03% 11.95%
Maine 1178 MH shipped	+ 45.61%	12wide — 96.54%	Doublewides — 2.85% Expandables — .61%	1. 60-64' 12wide 2. 50-54' 12wide 3. 65-69' 12wide	64.02% 19.92% 4.47%
Massachusetts 560 MH shipped	+ 20.69%	10wide — .85% 12wide — 85.47%	Doublewides — 4.28% Expandables — 8.55% Miscellaneous — .85%	1. 60-64' 12wide 2. 50-54' 12wide 3. Expandables	55.13% 15.81% 8.55%
New Hampshire 907 MH shipped	+ 21.74%	10wide — .26% 12wide — 94.24%	Doublewides — 4.19% Expandables — 1.31%	1. 60-64' 12wide 2. 50-54' 12wide 3. 70' & over 12wide	63.87% 19.90% 4.45%
Rhode Island 61 MH shipped	+ 27.08%	12wide — 100.00%		1. 60-64' 12wide 2. 50-54' 12wide 3. 40-44' 12wide	57.69% 34.61% 3.85%
Vermont 895 MH shipped	+ 50.67%	8wide — .53% 12wide — 97.09%	Doublewides — 2.12% Expandables — .26%	1. 60-64' 12wide 2. 50-54' 12wide 3. 65-69' 12wide	66.93% 19.84% 3.70%
TOTAL MH shipped — 4136			% of Total Projection — 3.66%		

WEST NORTH CENTRAL	% INCREASE % DECREASE	PRODUCT MIX	MOST POPULAR MODELS
Iowa 979 MH shipped	+ 24.87%	8wide — .24% 12wide — 89.51% Doublewides — 8.05% Expandables — 2.20%	1. 60-64' 12wide 59.76% 2. 50-54' 12wide 14.39% 3. 65-69' 12wide 8.29%
Kansas 1312 MH shipped	+ 7.10%	12wide — 78.69% Doublewides — 20.04% Expandables — 1.27%	1. 60-64' 12wide 45.72% 2. 50-54' 12wide 22.40% 3. Doublewides 12wide 15.12%
Minnesota 2106 MH shipped	+ 39.47%	8wide — .45% 10wide — 2.50% 12wide — 89.21% 14wide — 2.73% Doublewides — 3.07% Expandables — 1.36% Miscellaneous — .68%	1. 60-64' 12wide 59.66% 2. 50-54' 12wide 13.41% 3. 65-69' 12wides 8.41%
Missouri 2366 MH shipped	+ 42.27%	8wide — .20% 10wide — .10% 12wide — 85.46% Doublewides — 11.03% Expandables — 2.71% Miscellaneous — .50%	1. 60-64' 12wide 54.66% 2. 50-54' 12wide 19.46% 3. 40-44' 12wide 4.81%
Nebraska 926 MH shipped	+ 7.80%	12wide — 75.52% Doublewides — 19.33% Expandables — 2.32% Miscellaneous — 2.83%	1. 60-64' 12wide 39.18% 2. 50-54' 12wide 21.91% 3. Doublewides 12wide 13.66%
North Dakota 343 MH shipped	+ 27.51%	12wide — 75.69% 14wide — 5.56% Doublewides — 11.11% Expandables — 5.56% Miscellaneous — 2.08%	1. 60-64' 12wide 50.69% 2. 50-54' 12wide 14.58% 3. Doublewides 12wide 9.03%
South Dakota 993 MH shipped	+ 80.22%	12wide — 84.58% 14wide — 3.37% Doublewides — 10.84% Expandables — .73% Miscellaneous — .48%	1. 60-64' 12wide 44.58% 2. 50-54' 12wide 22.41% 3. 69-69' 12wide 8.67%

TOTAL MH shipped — 9025

% of Total Projection — 7.98%

VIRGIN ISLANDS	% INCREASE % DECREASE	PRODUCT MIX		MOST POPULAR MODELS
Virgin Islands 7 MH shipped	+100%	12wide — 100.00%		1. 60-64' 12wide 100.00%

% of Total Projection — .02%

TOTAL MH shipped — 7

MID-ATLANTIC	% INCREASE % DECREASE	PRODUCT MIX		MOST POPULAR MODELS
New Jersey 664 MH shipped	+ 37.75%	10wide — .72% 12wide — 92.44% 14wide — .36%	Doublewides — 1.08% Expandables — 2.88% Miscellaneous — 2.52%	1. 60-64' 12wide 61.15% 2. 50-54' 12wide 21.94% 3. 55-59' 12wide 3.60%
New York 4700 MH shipped	+ 20.27%	8wide — .05% 10wide — .20% 12wide — 94.86%	Doublewides — 3.36% Expandables — .71% Miscellaneous — .82%	1. 60-64' 12wide 66.00% 2. 50-54' 12wide 14.10% 3. 65-69' 12wide 7.58%
Pennsylvania 5885 MH shipped	+ 46.87%	8wide — .04% 10wide — .24% 12wide — 94.57%	Doublewide — 3.53% Expandables — 1.38% Miscellaneous — .24%	1. 60-64' 12wide 69.60% 2. 50-54' 12wide 14.41% 3. 65-69' 12wide 4.02%

% of Total Projection — 9.95%

TOTAL MH shipped — 11,249

THE INDUSTRY

WEST SOUTH CENTRAL

State	% INCREASE / % DECREASE	PRODUCT MIX		MOST POPULAR MODELS
Arkansas 1352 MH shipped	+ 61.34%	8wide — .17% 12wide — 94.73%	Doublewides — 4.75% Expandables — .35%	1. 60-64' 12wide 44.11% 2. 50-54' 12wide 25.13% 3. 40-44' 12wide 18.80%
Louisiana 1968 MH shipped	+ 22.69%	8wide — 2.55% 12wide — 88.96%	Doublewides — 7.16% Expandables — .97% Miscellaneous — .36%	1. 60-64' 12wide 49.51% 2. 50-54' 12wide 20.99% 3. 40-44' 12wide 12.01%
Oklahoma 2192 MH shipped	+ 66.19%	8wide — 1.31% 12wide — 92.06% 14wide — 1.52%	Doublewides — 3.81% Expandables — .87% Miscellaneous — .43%	1. 60-64' 12wide 54.30% 2. 50-54' 12wide 21.98% 3. 40-44' 12wide 8.60%
Texas 6781 MH shipped	+ 46.81%	8wide — 1.37% 12wide — 88.99% 14wide — 2.11%	Doublewides — 2.18% Expandables — 1.16% Miscellaneous — 4.19%	1. 60-64' 12wide 54.57% 2. 50-54' 12wide 20.62% 3. 40-44' 12wide 7.53%

TOTAL MH shipped — 12,293   % of Total Projection — 10.88%

EAST SOUTH CENTRAL

State	% INCREASE / % DECREASE	PRODUCT MIX		MOST POPULAR MODELS
Alabama 3136 MH shipped	+ 57.11%	10wide — .83% 12wide — 97.12%	Doublewides — .38% Expandables — 1.14% Miscellaneous — .53%	1. 60-64' 12wide 55.34% 2. 50-54' 12wide 21.38% 3. 40-44' 12wide 13.72%
Kentucky 1572 MH shipped	+ 24.56%	8wide — .30% 10wide — 3.03% 12wide — 92.44%	Doublewides — 3.63% Expandables — .60%	1. 60-64' 12wide 54.31% 2. 50-54' 12wide 26.17% 3. 40-44' 12wide 6.35%
Mississippi 1710 MH shipped	+ 21.10%	8wide — 1.11% 10wide — .41% 12wide — 90.44%	Doublewides — 2.08% Expandables — 2.08% Miscellaneous — 3.88%	1. 60-64' 12wide 49.58% 2. 50-54' 12wide 23.96% 3. 40-44' 12wide 13.71%
Tennessee 2480 MH shipped	+ 29.37%	10wide — .19% 12wide — 96.74%	Doublewides — 2.30% Expandables — .67% Miscellaneous — .10%	1. 60-64' 12wide 53.83% 2. 50-54' 12wide 21.65% 3. 40-44' 12wide 13.03%

TOTAL MH shipped — 8898   % of Total Projection — 7.87%

MOUNTAIN STATES	% INCREASE % DECREASE	PRODUCT MIX		MOST POPULAR MODELS
Arizona 1655 MH shipped	+ 84.91%	10wide — 1.72% 12wide — 78.05% 14wide — .86%	Doublewide — 17.79% Miscellaneous — 1.58%	1. 60-64' 12wide 51.79% 2. 50-54' 12wide 15.49% 3. Doublewides 12wide 14.63%
Colorado 1512 MH shipped	− 4.96%	8wide — .32% 12wide — 75.39%	Doublewide — 16.88% Expandables — 5.20% Miscellaneous — 2.21%	1. 60-64' 12wide 46.69% 2. 50-54' 12wide 14.20% 3. Doublewides 12wide 12.78%
Idaho 867 MH shipped	+ 34.83%	8wide — .55% 12wide — 86.78%	Doublewides — 11.57% Expandables — 1.10%	1. 60-64' 12wide 66.12% 2. 50-54' 12wide 12.68% 3. Doublewides 12wide 5.51%
Montana 947 MH shipped	+ 34.51%	12wide — 78.70% 14wide — 2.25%	Doublewides — 12.78% Expandables — 2.51% Miscellaneous — 3.76%	1. 60-64' 12wide 48.12% 2. 50-54' 12wide 13.03% 3. Doublewides 12wide 11.28%
Nevada 871 MH shipped	+ 67.50%	10wide — .27% 12wide — 86.54%	Doublewides — 11.54% Expandables — 1.65%	1. 60-64' 12wide 63.74% 2. 50-54' 12wide 18.41% 3. Doublewides 12wide 6.87%
New Mexico 598 MH shipped	− 10.07%	12wide — 88.09% 14wide — 2.78%	Doublewides — 7.54% Expandables — 1.19% Miscellaneous — .40%	1. 60-64' 12wide 61.51% 2. 50-54' 12wide 14.28% 3. 40-44' 12wide 4.76%

Utah
295 MH shipped — + 31.11%

12wide — 86.29%	Doublewides — 10.49%	1. 60-64' 12wide 63.71%
	Expandables — 1.61%	2. 50-54' 12wide 16.13%
	Miscellaneous — 1.61%	3. Doublewides 12wide 5.65%

Wyoming
413 MH shipped — + 69.96%

12wide — 85.55%	Doublewides — 7.51%	1. 60-64' 12wide 56.65%
14wide — .58%	Expandables — 4.05%	2. 50-54' 12wide 16.18%
	Miscellaneous — 2.31%	3. 65-69' 12wide 9.25%

% of Total Projection — 6.33%

TOTAL MH shipped — 7158

PACIFIC	% INCREASE % DECREASE	PRODUCT MIX		MOST POPULAR MODELS
California 6546 MH shipped	+ 32.86%	10wide — 1.63% 12wide — 57.97%	Doublewides — 39.28% Expandables — .69% Miscellaneous — .43%	1. 60-64' 12wide 37.11% 2. Doublewides 12wide 26.23% 3. 50-54' 12wide 14.81%
Hawaii				
Oregon 2017 MH shipped	+ 18.93%	10wide — .59% 12wide — 77.00%	Doublewides — 20.17% Expandables — 2.24%	1. 60-64' 12wide 55.19% 2. 50-54' 12wide 14.62% 3. Doublewides 12wide 10.38%
Washington 3088 MH shipped	+ 19.60%	8wide — .23% 10wide — .38% 12wide — 79.54%	Doublewides — 17.62% Expandables — 2.23%	1. 60-64' 12wide 58.00% 2. 50-54' 12wide 12.92% 3. Doublewides 12wide 9.69%

% of Total Projection — 10.31%

TOTAL MH shipped — 11,651

Courtesy: Kanzol Sportrailer

up and
down

Courtesy: Bethany Trailers

Courtesy: Jayco

Courtesy: Sunset Traveler, Inc.

Typical tent camping trailers.

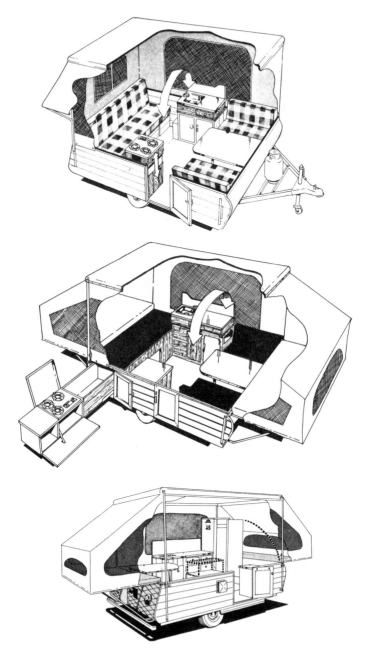

Courtesy: *Wheel Camper Corp.*

Tent camping trailers come in many models.

51

pickup truck, and when not in use, they are easily removed and parked on special jacks. Medium sized units are carried on three-quarter-ton or larger trucks, depending on weight and size. The chassis-mount type of truck camper is permanently affixed directly to the truck frame.

Retail prices start at about $1,000 and range up to $4,000, and higher, for luxury units. This recreational vehicle accounted for 31.38 percent of the 1968 production of recreational vehicles.

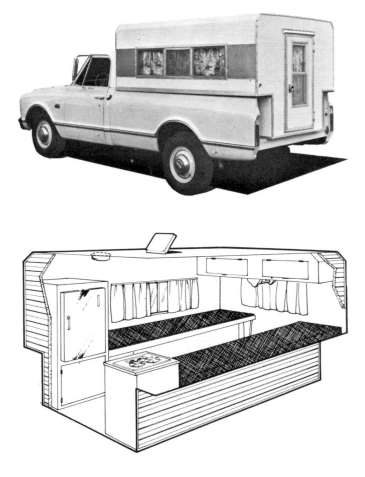

A low priced slide-in camper.

Courtesy: Honorbuilt Division of Ward Mfg. Co.
Top two pictures are slide-in camper. Bottom picture is a chassis mount camper.

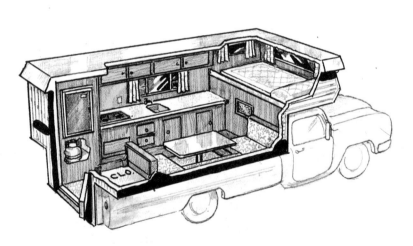

Courtesy: Champion Home Builders Co.
Exterior and interior view of a popular size truck camper.

Courtesy: Kit Mfg. Co.

Exterior and interior of an 8½ foot Kit camper.

Travel Trailers

Travel trailers are vehicular structures mounted on wheels .Two or four wheels are used, depending on the size and weight. They do not require special highway movement permits when towed by an automobile or truck. They are the most popular type of recreational vehicle in use; 1968 production represented 40.31 percent of the recreational vehicle market. Travel trailers are available in a wide range of sizes from compact 12' models up to luxury completely self-contained 35'. Prices start at around $700 and go to $10,000, or higher, for deluxe units.

Motor Homes

Motor homes are self-powered. Many consider them the ultimate in travel and recreational vehicle use. They are built on a truck or bus chassis and are usually self-contained. They measure up to 30' to length and vary in cost from slightly under $5,000 to over $20,000, depending on the features the buyer wishes. In 1968 motor homes represented 4.55 percent of the recreational vehicle market. This type of recreational vehicle, however, seems to be increasing in popularity.

Recreational Vehicle Industry Growth

We have published below statistical information concerning the growth of the recreational vehicle industry.

One additional matter needs to be mentioned for a full understanding of the recreational vehicle market. This is the matter of self-containment. Many recreational vehicles are classified as self-contained which means that the vehicle contains everything needed for living, days at a time, without hooking up to outside electricity or plumbing. The deluxe units require the traveler to visit a sanitary station to dispose of waste and replace fresh water only approximately once a week. Such units have complete cooking facilities, lights, refrigerations, toilets, showers, and carry their own gas supply for cooking and heating, and in some cases for lighting. Some have hot and cold running water, and sometimes electric generators for lights, refrigeration, and other power appliances. Often they are equipped with 12-volt electrical systems which are easily converted to 110-volt systems when

Courtesy: Shasta Trailers
Exterior and interior views of a small travel trailer.

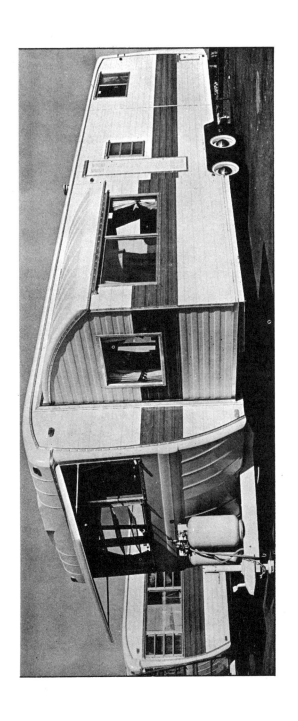

Courtesy: Ken-craft

Some travel trailers expand in size when parked.

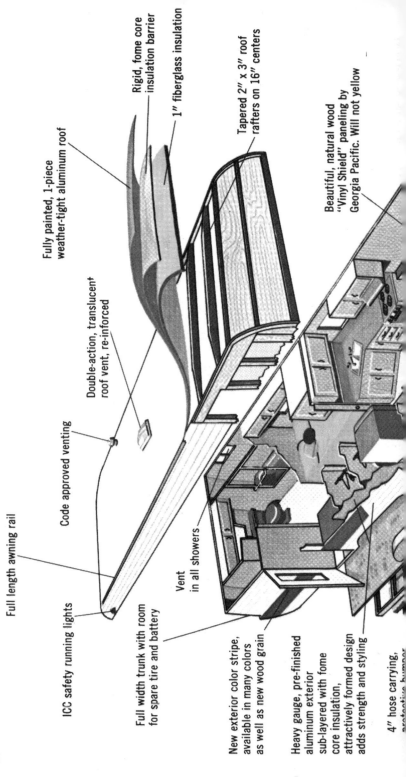

Rigid, fome core insulation barrier

1" fiberglass insulation

Fully painted, 1-piece weather-tight aluminum roof

Tapered 2" x 3" roof rafters on 16" centers

Beautiful, natural wood "Vinyl Shield" paneling by Georgia Pacific. Will not yellow

Double-action, translucent roof vent, re-inforced

Code approved venting

Full length awning rail

Vent in all showers

ICC safety running lights

Full width trunk with room for spare tire and battery

New exterior color stripe, available in many colors as well as new wood grain

Heavy gauge, pre-finished aluminum exterior sub-layered with fome core insulation, attractively formed design adds strength and styling

4" hose carrying, protective bumper

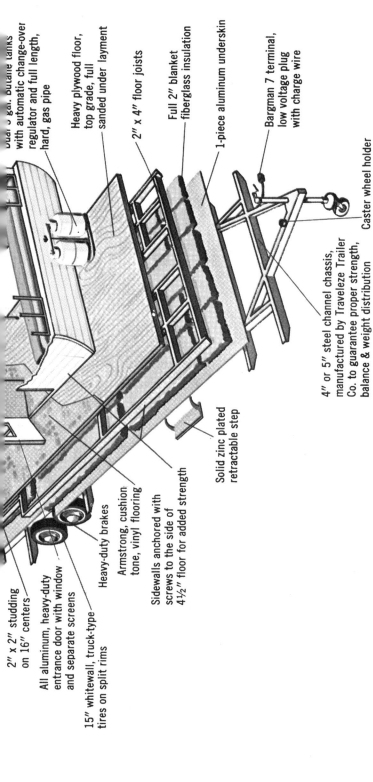

Dual 5 gal. butane tanks with automatic change-over regulator and full length, hard, gas pipe

Heavy plywood floor, top grade, full sanded under layment

2" x 4" floor joists

Full 2" blanket fiberglass insulation

1-piece aluminum underskin

Bargman 7 terminal, low voltage plug with charge wire

Caster wheel holder

4" or 5" steel channel chassis, manufactured by Traveleze Trailer Co. to guarantee proper strength, balance & weight distribution

Solid zinc plated retractable step

Sidewalls anchored with screws to the side of 4½" floor for added strength

Armstrong, cushion tone, vinyl flooring

Heavy-duty brakes

15" whitewall, truck-type tires on split rims

All aluminum, heavy-duty entrance door with window and separate screens

2" x 2" studding on 16" centers

Courtesy: Traveleze Trailer Company

Travel trailers are built to rigid construction standards. In some states construction standards are state controlled.

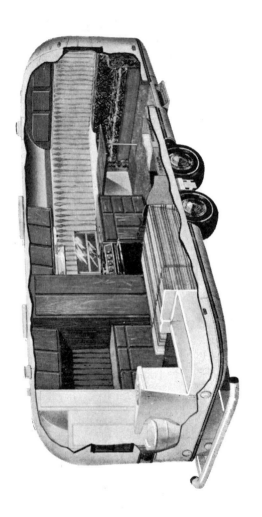

Courtesy: Avion Coach Corp.

Interior view of an Avion travel trailer.

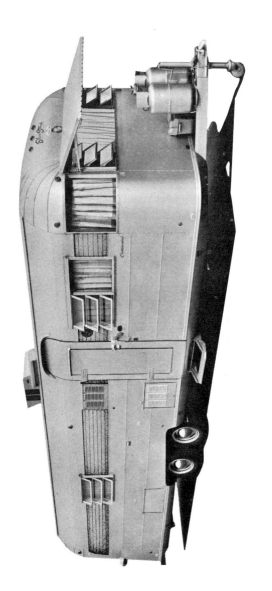

Courtesy: Silver Streak

A deluxe 32 foot aircraft type construction travel trailer.

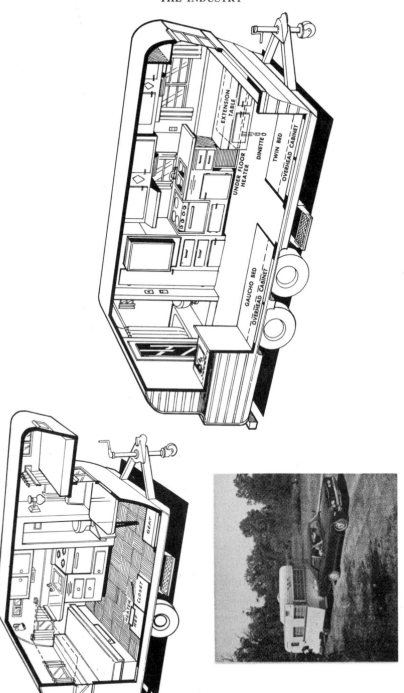

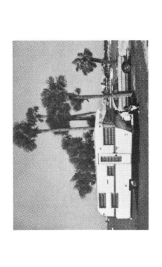

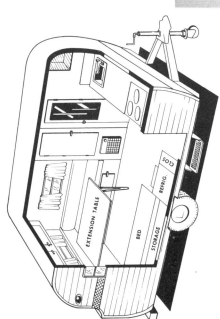

Courtesy: Monitor Coach Co.

Some exterior and interior views of Monitor travel trailers.

Courtesy: Avco Corp.
Some travel trailers are collapsible to reduce wind resistance when being towed.

67

A large motor home.

Courtesy: Travel Car Division, United Bus Sales, Inc.

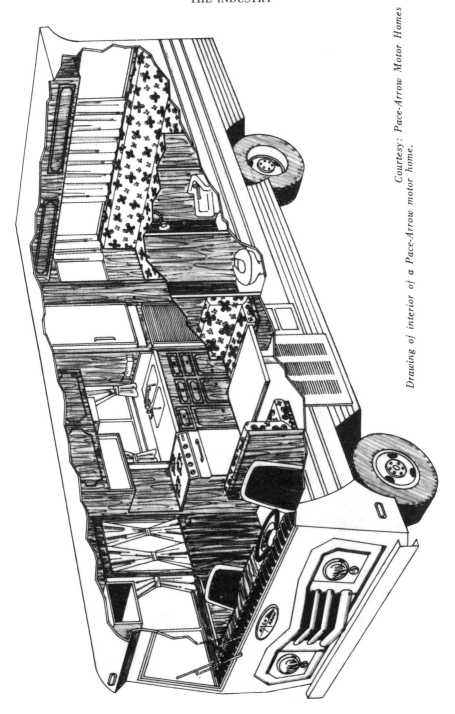

Drawing of interior of a Pace-Arrow motor home.

Courtesy: Pace-Arrow Motor Homes

Exterior and interior photos of Shasta motor homes.

Courtesy: *Shasta Trailers*

71

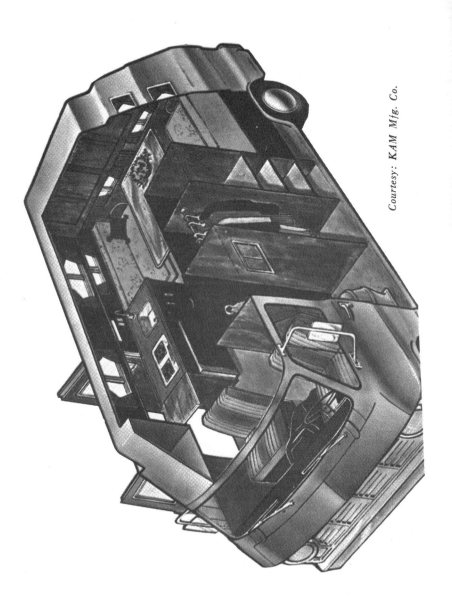

Courtesys Motor Homes Inc.

Courtesy: Red-E-Kamp Inc.

Converted vans are recreational vehicles too.

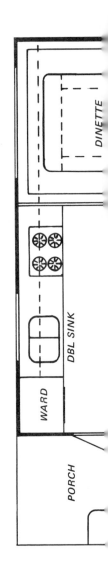

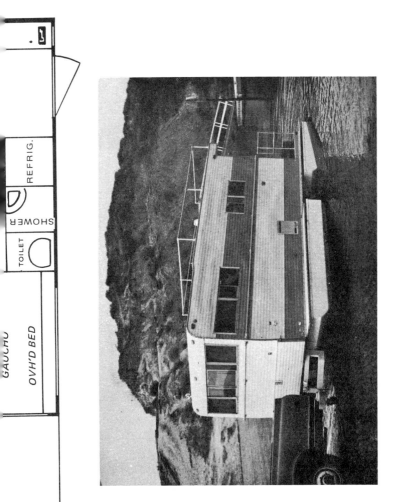

Courtesy: Aqua-Trail Inc.

An amphibious recreational vehicle.

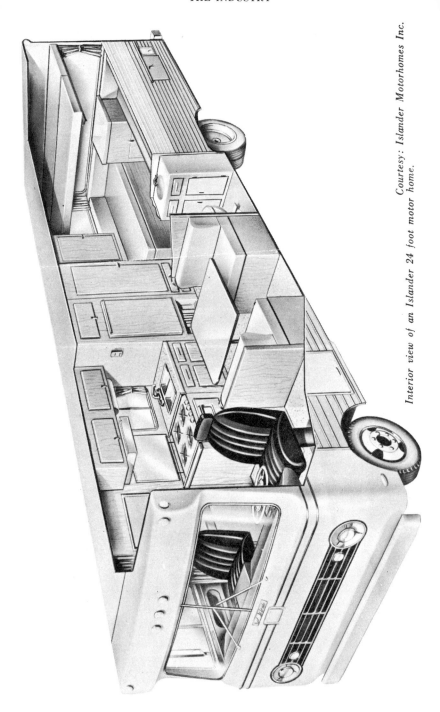

Courtesy: Islander Motorhomes Inc.

Interior view of an Islander 24 foot motor home.

outside power hookups are available.

The Park Industry

The park industry may be classified into two divisions: the mobile home park and the recreational vehicle park.

To some extent the two classifications are not exclusive: there are a limited number of parks which are predominately built for recreational vehicles but which also have a mobile home section; and there are a considerable number of mobile home parks which accept some recreational vehicles. It is

RECREATIONAL VEHICLE SHIPMENTS

Travel Trailer Shipments:

Year	Units Shipped	Estimated Retail Value
1968	161,530	$500,743,000
1967	132,540	304,842,000
1966	122,700	282,210,000
1965	107,580	236,676,000
1964	90,370	162,656,000
1963	73,370	132,066,000
1962	58,200	105,000,000
1961	40,500	73,000,000
1960	40,300	73,000,000
1959	42,000	75,000,000
1958	31,750	57,000,000
1957	24,200	43,000,000
1956	15,370	28,000,000

Unit Shipments — Other Recreational Vehicles:

Year	Truck Coach	Camping Trailers	Motor Homes
1968	125,760	95,220	18,220
1967	97,110	79,280	12,500
1966	75,300	86,300	
1965	67,220	70,000	
1964	52,000	55,000	
1963	40,300	42,500	
1962	23,000	26,500	
1961	18,000	25,000	

Source: Mobile Home Manufacturers Association and the Recreational Vehicle Institute.

not uncommon for new mobile home parks to accept recreational vehicles on an overnight or weekly basis until such time as the park has filled with regular mobile home tenants.

Mobile Home Parks

There are approximately 22,000 mobile home parks in the United States, but according to one of the industry's leading directories, *Woodall's Mobile Home Park Directory*, published by the Woodall Publishing Company, 500 Hyacinth Place, Highland Park, Illinois 60035, only 13,000 of these parks were of sufficient quality as to warrant being listed in their 1969 Directory. That directory covered approximately 800,000 mobile home sites. Mobile home parks in the past have averaged from 60 to 75 sites, but the modern development runs from 150 to 300 sites. According to the Mobile Home Manufacturer's Association of Chicago, Illinois, the national average vacancy rate in 1968 for mobile home parks was 4.2 percent. Monthly park rental rates range from $25 per month up to several hundred dollars per month in a few select and very luxurious parks. The average monthly rate would be around $45 per month. In areas where modern, deluxe mobile home communities are currently being developed it is not unusual to see rental rates averaging $65 to $85 per month. Such mobile home communities are, however, deluxe; the meaning of this term will become clearer as you proceed further into this book. Mobile home park development costs vary from $1000 to $3000 per space, exclusive of the cost of the land. The wide variation is due to the geographical location and costs in the community plus the degree of sophistication which is built into the park. Thus, in some cases a park is developed on the basis of little more than clearing a land area and putting in oiled gravel roads, partitioning off lots for development. In other cases a deluxe community is established with all types of recreational facilities.

Mobile home parks have tended to be established on land on the periphery of well-populated areas. Such location has been selected due to the low cost of the land, making possible low rental rates. As a city grows the park property usually becomes extremely valuable, resulting in the sale of the land for other purposes. Newly developed parks have then moved to the outskirts of the community, again for reasons of land cost. As the mobile home itself has become larger in size, so has the lot on which the mobile home is parked. Recommended number of sites per acre has come down from 18 to 15 per acre in past years to a present level of 7- to 8-sites to the acre. Although there has been considerable community opposition to mobile home parks in the past, there is a growing acceptance of this type of community due to the upgrading of both the mobile home and the park facilities to make it competitive with the conventional housing development. A typical mobile home community at the present time runs approximately 7 or 8 spaces to the acre, is beautifully landscaped, has paved streets, sidewalks, underground utilities, off-street parking, playgrounds, swimming pool, recreation building, and all types of additional recreational facilities.

Recreational Vehicle Parks

Recreational vehicle parks, like mobile home parks, are built in all sizes and shapes, with varying accommodations. Some are quite rustic, capitalizing on the beauty of the surrounding scenic area; some, catering to overnighters, will be the essence of simplicity; and others, catering to vacationers who wish to spend a week or more in a place, will be deluxe in every respect.

The Woodall Publishing Company, mentioned previously, publishes a *Trailering Parks and Campgrounds Directory*, in addition to its *Mobile Home Park Directory*.

The directory indicates that in 1968 there were 15,302 parks and campgrounds accepting campers and recreational vehicles in the United States. They had 444,424 camp sites. Of these, 9,591 campgrounds were privately owned, and these privavtely owned campgrounds had 267,424 camp sites. The remaining 5,711 parks were operated by various branches of the federal, state, and local government, and they encompassed 177,000 sites. The top 14 states, from the point of view of number of camp sites, are detailed in the table below, reprinted through the courtesy of the Woodall Publishing Company.

TOP 14 STATES — U.S.A.

ACCORDING TO TOTAL CAMPSITES

State	Private Campgrounds		Public Campgrounds		Total Campsites
	Parks	Campsites	Parks	Campsites	
California	1,142	24,098	783	19,690	43,788
New York	373	30,812	88	9,115	29,927
Michigan	330	12,286	305	16,540	28,826
Wisconsin	546	23,036	105	4,743	27,779
Washington	455	20,755	359	7,766	20,655
Florida	748	16,874	69	3,013	16,874
Illinois	137	16,140	75	7,187	16,140
Arizona	407	12,031	116	3,083	15,114
Ohio	248	7,398	60	7,197	14,595
Colorado	219	5,810	289	6,246	12,056
Maine	200	10,412	41	1,265	11,677
Texas	393	7,903	175	3,336	11,239
Pennsylvania	265	7,261	48	3,523	10,784
Wyoming	108	6,287	130	4,769	10,056

Courtesy: Woodall Publishing Co.

The Woodall organization rates camp sites in their annual directory based upon personal inspection of each site by their traveling representatives. In the table which follows we have shown a breakdown of the rating of privately owned parks for recreational vehicles in the United States, according to the rating method used by the Woodall organization. Those campgrounds which have limited facilities have been inspected and found to have pure water, pit toilets, a lighted area, and reasonable access. Those which are rated *fair* have, in addition, electrical hookups, frequent water taps, showers (which may be cold), and recreation in the immediate vicinity or have a scenic location. Those rated as *good* will have, in addition, flush toilets, hot showers, a dumping station, adequate tables, good recreation, setting, management, appearance, and access. Those parks which are rated *excellent* provide some full hookups, or multiple dumping stations within easy reach of campsites, excellent toilet and shower facilities, some grocery stores on site, recreation, including swimming, a recreation hall or pavilion, hard-surfaced roads, excellent setting, appearance, and management.

QUALITY OF U.S. PRIVATELY OWNED CAMPSITES

	Not Rated	Limited Facilities	Fair	Good	Excellent
PARKS	1,952	1,216	4,164	1,856	403
SITES	49,833	3,779	88,044	87,708	38,060

For description of "Limited", "Fair", "Good" and "Excellent" see paragraph preceeding table.

Courtesy: Woodall Publishing Co.

Recreational vehicle parks are located along main highways or in areas where there are particular recreational attractions. When located near state, county, or federal parks they are to some extent competitive with the features offered by the publicly owned parks. Rates tend to be higher than those in public facilities because the parks usually offer superior accommodations. Overnight rates may run from $2 to $8 a night depending upon the accommodations. Weekly and monthly rates are frequently also offered. Construction costs for such parks run from very minimal cost of a few hundred dollars per space to as much as several thousand dollars per space for deluxe accommodations. The size of spaces offered in recreational vehicle parks varies with the type clientele that is expected. Densities may run as high as 20 per acre.

Parks With Lots For Sale

A development in the mobile home park industry which seems to be accelerating is the development of a mobile home park where the site is owned by the resident rather than rented. In the conventional mobile home park the resident rents his space on a month to month basis subject to his adherence to the park's rules and regulations or his own desire to move elsewhere. The new development markets mobile home parks sites either on the condominum principle or on the subdivision basis with various restrictions in the deed which, in effect, become the rules and regulations of the park. Lots in such developments sell for from $500 to several thousand dollars per space depending upon the value of the land and the amount of development put into the project before the mobile home owner is sold the lot. Frequently the situation is similar to that of a home owner buying a lot and constructing a house on it. Merely the bare lot is provided with the roads being in and the utilities coming to the site. The mobile home owner must develop his own site at his own cost. The more successful operations of this type have been those which were built around the condominium principle because there is more continuity of management. When lots are sold on a sub-division basis with deed restrictions, there tends to be a deterioration in management as soon as the sub-division has been completely sold.

On the pages which follow we have printed numerous pictures taken in mobile home and recreational vehicle parks to better orient the reader to the subject being discussed.

Park Classification and Facilities

Parks are often classified according to the type of residents they accept. The facilities the park offers its residents in turn are related to the size of the park, type of residents, and rental rates.

Immediately above we have discussed facilities offered

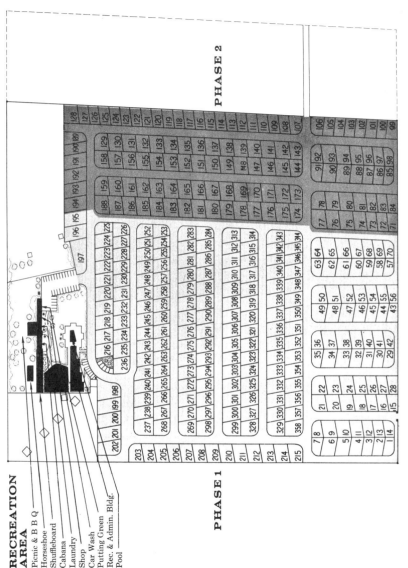

Plot plan for a 344 space Southern California park.

RECREATION AREA

- Picnic & B B Q
- Horseshoe
- Shuffleboard
- Cabana
- Laundry
- Shop
- Car Wash
- Putting Green
- Rec. & Admin. Bldg.
- Pool

PHASE 1

PHASE 2

Artist's drawing of a Southern California mobile home park.

Scene from a Tampa, Florida mobile home park.

Courtesy: Guernsey City

A recreational vehicle park planned for Anaheim, California.

Partial view of an ocean front Southern California mobile home park. Recreation room is in foreground.

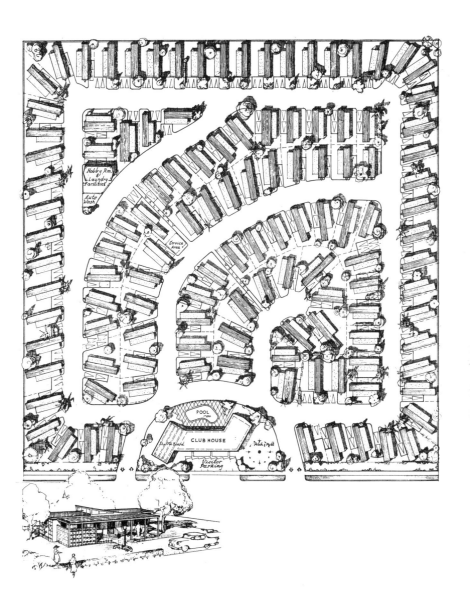

Plot plan for a 117 space mobile home community.

Courtesy: M & R Housing Merchandiser
Swimming pool in a recreational vehicle park.

Courtesy: M & R Housing Merchandiser
Central building of a recreational park in Missouri.

Central building for a recreational vehicle park associated with the Kamp Dakota chain.

Courtesy: M & R Housing Merchandiser

Rancho Escondido, Escondido, Calif.

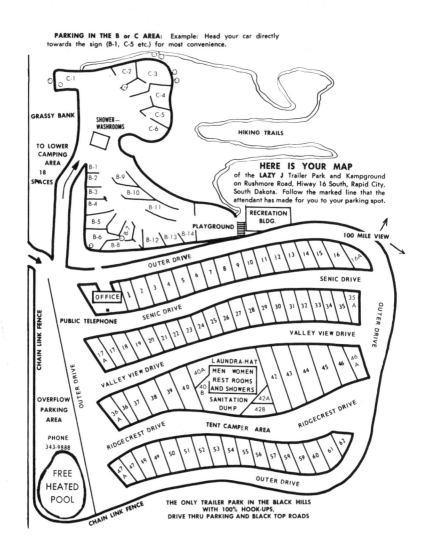

Layout of the Lazy J Trailer Park and Kampground, Rapid City, South Dakota.

Courtesy: SkyeRise Terrace, Inc.

For the future . . . a multi-story mobile home park.

Street scene of a Colton, California mobile home park.

Courtesy: Willow Lake Estates, Elgin, Illinois
In large parks, service facilities such as laundry rooms, card rooms, rest rooms, baths, etc., are often spotted at convenient locations about the park in addition to the main, large, centrally located recreation facilities.

Courtesy: Guernsey City, Tampa, Florida
This setting is typical of the atmosphere in today's modern mobile home park.

94

Courtesy: Solana y Sombra Trailer Estates, Tucson, Arizona
Note layout and landscaping of this popular mobile home park in Tucson, Arizona.

Courtesy: Green Acres Mobile Home Estates, Anaheim, California
Beautiful modern and complete recreation facilities are a central feature of
Green Acres Mobile Home Estates.

Courtesy: Guernsey City, Tampa, Florida

Attractive landscaping is a dominant feature in modern parks.

97

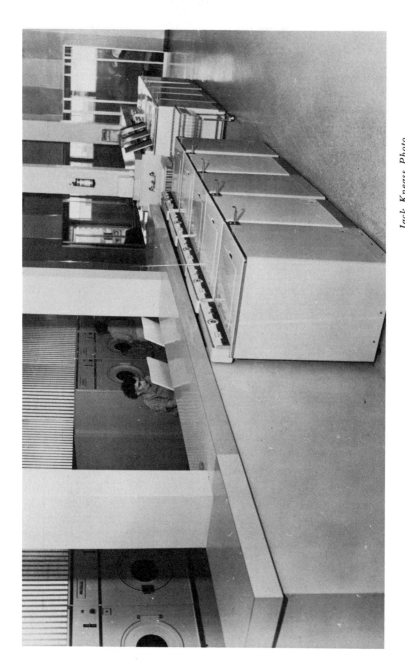

Jack Kneass Photo

Laundry facilities at Belmore Shores Mobile Estates, Long Beach, Calif.

View of community kitchen, part of the recreation room in a modern mobile home park.

Jack Kneass Photo

Jack Kneass Photos

Modern mobile home parks have attractively designed recreation rooms.

Entrance hall of a recreation building in a Southern California park.

Jack Kneass Photo

Courtesy: Guernsey City
Photos on this and the following few pages show recreation facilities and activities in modern mobile home parks.

Jack Kneass Photo

Jack Kneass Photo

Jack Kneass Photo

Jack Kneass Photo

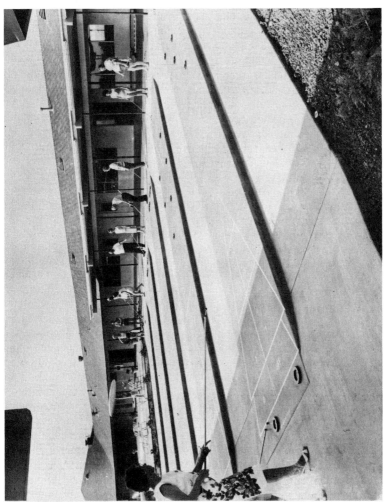

by recreational vehicle parks. Let us turn our attention now to mobile home park classifications and a discussion of mobile home park facilities.

A typical classification of mobile home parks according to residents would be as follows.

Retirement Parks. Residents do not have full time employment and usually must qualify in age as a senior citizen. Such parks emphasize social and recreational programs.

Adult Parks. Residents are restricted to families with no minor children. Residents are usually employed in the local labor market.

Service Personnel Parks. Residents are military personnel. Such parks are located close to the military base which employs the park residents. Civilian employees of the military are also permitted residents.

Construction Project Parks. Residents are employed at a nearby major construction project. Such parks usually go out of business when the project is completed, having been built to provide housing for the project's workers.

Family Parks. Accept residents with children. Working members of the family are employed in the local labor market.

Student Park. Residents are both single and married students attending a nearby educational institution. Children are permitted.

Second Home Parks. Such parks are located in a resort area. Residents are "temporary" in the sense that their permanent home is located elsewhere; they visit their "second-home" on weekends, holidays and on special occasions.

Mixed Parks. Often a park will take several classes of residents. Usually an effort is made to keep similar residents in the same area of the park. Thus a park which takes both families with children and those without children will have a section of the park set aside for each type of resident.

There is a large variation in the type of facilities which parks offer. The Woodall Publishing Company publishes a directory of U.S. Mobile Home Parks in which it rates parks as 1, 2, 3, 4 or 5 Star Parks. We have reprinted below the criteria Woodall uses for their rating to give the reader comprehensive knowledge of park facilities.

Woodall One Star Park

The most important consideration for a one star park is overall appearance. If it is not a decent place to live, it will not be listed in Woodall's Directory.

The following are general requirements:

Fair overall appearance.

Patios on most lots. May be concrete, asphalt, wood, or some suitable material.

Grass, rock or shell to cover ground.

Streets fair to good. May be dirt, asphalt or gravel in reasonable condition.

Restrooms clean, if any.

Adequate laundry or laundromat nearby.

If fences allowed, must be neat.

Mail service.

Homes may be old models but show evidence of care.

Manager available some hours of each day.

Woodall Two Star Park

In addition to the requirements for a one star park, a two star park will have the following:

Landscaping — some lawns and shrubs.

Streets in good condition. Must be dust free of crushed rock, gravel or shell minimum.

Neat storage.

Well equipped laundry or laundromat nearby.

220 volt connections available.

If children accepted, park should have play area.

Park free of clutter, such as old cars and other abandoned equipment.

Well maintained and managed.

Woodall Three Star Park

What a three star park does it does well but not as uniformly as higher rated parks. Many three star parks were once higher rated, but original construction does not allow for today's 10-foot, 12-foot, and double-wides or the 55-foot and 60-foot lengths. If children are allowed, there should be adequate play area. However, the disarray caused by children may at times be the determining factor that keeps a three star park at that level when it otherwise could be rated higher.

In addition to the requirements for a one and two star park, a three star park must have the following:

Attractive entrance.

All mobile homes must be in good condition.

Awnings and cabana rooms on some homes in southern areas.

Some spaces for large mobile homes.

Paved or hard surfaced streets.

Off-street parking or streets wide enough for safe on-street parking.

Good lawns or substitute throughout, shade trees, some shrubs where climate permits.

Concrete patios or the equivalent on all lots.

All lots neat and attractive.

All park buildings in good repair.

Good management.

Woodall Four Star Park

Four star parks are luxury parks. In addition to the requirements for a one, two and three star park a four star park must have the following:

Good landscaping.

Most homes skirted with metal skirts, concrete block, ornamental wood or stone.

Paved streets, edged or curbed.

Uncrowded lots.

Underground utilities if permitted by local conditions and authorities.

Most tanks, if present, concealed.

Any hedges or fences must be attractive and uniform.

Awnings, cabanas, or porches on most homes in southern areas. (Excepting double-wide units.)

Most lots to accommodate large mobile homes.

Where row parking of homes exists, all must be lined up uniformly.

Community hall and/or swimming pool and/or recreation program. If a park is four star in all but this requirement, the fourth star will be printed as an open star indicating a four star park without park-centered recreation. Excellent management.

Woodall Five Star Park

Five star parks are the finest. They should be nearly impossible to improve. In addition to the requirements for a one, two, three, and four star park, a five star park must have the following:

Well planned and laid out spacious appearance.

Good location in regard to accessibility and desirable neighborhood. In some locations park should be enclosed by high hedges or ornamental fence.

Wide paved streets in perfect condition. Curbs or lawns edged to streets, sidewalks, street lights, street signs.

Homes set back from street.

Exceptionally attractive entrance and park sign.

Patios at least 8 x 30 ft. (Excepting double-wide units.)

Paved off-street parking such as carports or planned parking.

All homes skirted.

All hitches concealed. Any existing tanks concealed.

Recreation, some or all of the following: swimming pool (excepting areas with long, cold winters), shuffleboards, horseshoe pitching, golf course, hobby shop, hobby classes, games, potlucks, dances or natural recreational facilities.

Beautifully equipped recreation hall with kitchen. Room for community gatherings, tiled restrooms, etc.

Uniform storage sheds or central storage facilities.

All late model homes in excellent condition.

At least 60% occupancy in order to judge quality of residents which indicates park's ability to maintain a five star rating between inspections.

All empty lots grassed, graveled or otherwise well maintained.

If pets or children allowed, there must be a place for them to run and play without cluttering the streets and yards. *Most five star parks are for adults only.*

Superior management interested in comfort of residents and maintenance of park.

SUCCESS FACTORS

This book has been designed for those investigating the park industry for the purpose of considering investing either time, capital, or both in the park industry. This chapter has been placed in the book to help focus the reading in subsequent chapters and to bring into a single chapter a discussion of both the rewards and obstacles to successful investment in this industry.

The park industry is no more mysterious than any other. Its basic pattern for success is to discover a profitable location, prepare on that location a well-conceived plant, and finally to manage that plant well. These are the basic ingredients that go into the success of any enterprise of this type.

Those investigating the park industry will want to know how to locate and recognize a prime location, how to define an excellent plant, and how to establish policies leading to successful management. We will deal with all of these matters in their proper place.

Rewards For Park Management

The individual who invests his time in *operating* a park should be an individual who basically enjoys working with people. The manager of such an enterprise is like the mayor of a small city. Such individuals enjoy leadership, a busy life, recreation, lots of friends, excitement, accomplishment, fun, and a good income.

Investment Return

From an investor's point of view the park industry presently offers excellent return on investment. It appears that this will be so for some time to come. The frequent question put to those of us in the industry who specialize in the management and development of mobile home parks is "How much return can I get on my money?" It is grossly misleading to a prospective investor to quote an average return. After all, the return depends upon location, plant, and management. A conservative answer to such a question would be that the investor might expect a return far in excess of what he might expect from the ownership of stocks, bonds, or conventional real estate holdings — providing his investment is prudently made. The wise investor puts his money on the line only when a site has been evaluated by an authoritatively prepared feasibility study, when a competent park architect has been engaged, and when professional management has been assured.

Resale Profit

In addition to return on invested capital, evaluated in terms of annual rate of return on equity capital, there are additional benefits to an investor. One obvious benefit is the possibility of profit to be realized from the resale of the park. There is a world of difference between the value of a park built but unfilled and the value of a park full and producing a stable income stream. For this reason there is considerable profit in the resale of a park after it has been established with a good income stream for a period of time.

Land Appreciation

Another reward to the park investor is land appreciation, provided he builds his park on owned land rather than leased land. In this sense he is enjoying the same return as any other investor in land. The park industry, however, offers an unusual opportunity to enjoy land appreciation profits. Parks are often referred to as an interim land use. As mentioned before, parks are frequently located on the periphery of well-populated areas; as the population goes outward the value of the land increases. Because the mobile homes themselves are easily moved, the cost of clearing the land for future development is negligible.

Tax Shelter

The park industry also offers the investor the usual tax shelter connected with investments in real estate. Depreciation rates are higher than is the case of most real estate because the Bureau of Internal Revenue has as yet set no guide-lines. Furthermore, establishing guide-lines requiring a long period for depreciation would be most difficult in view of the fact that technological changes in the industry have caused parks which were built in the past to depreciate rather rapidly because of obsolescence.

The Location

Let us now discuss some of the obstacles encountered in developing good investment return in the park industry. We have mentioned above that the right location is one of the primary requisites of a successful park. One reason the park industry offers excellent return is that the location of a good site can be extremely difficult. This keeps competition to a minimum. Site location is no matter for a novice. Those who feel that simply because they own a piece of acreage it would be desirable to build a park are, in most cases, mistaken. The site for a successful park must be very carefully selected. This is one of the matters with which we shall deal in detail in a subsequent chapter.

Amount Of Capital Needed

The proper amount of equity capital is another important factor in a successful park. In the past, far too many have entered the industry with inadequate capital, only to expend the sums they have available and discover that they must sell out at a considerable loss to someone else who is able to take over and develop the park with sufficient capital. As a rule of thumb for those who are considering investment in the park industry, it would be wise for them, to compute the total cost of developing the park to completion (including land cost); from this sum deduct the amount of loans which can be obtained on a long term basis; to this residual should be added the cost of operating the park for a two year period including all mortgage payments, adequate working capital, and a contingency reserve fund; then, deduct from this sum the amount which will be realized in rents on the basis of a straight line filling of the park over a two year period. The example below will illustrate this point.

Assume: 40 acres costing $5,000 per acre is to be developed 8 spaces per acre to cost $2,500 per space to develop.

Rental rate $60.00 per month.

Takes 6 month to build park.

Park will fill on a linear basis in two years.

Construction loan for 1 year at 8% interest.

Long term loan of 80% of total cost at 8% interest and loan fee of 2 points — annual payment $79,680.

Annual operating cost excluding interest and depreciation is $74,000.

Then: 40 acres x 8 spaces = 320 spaces

40 acres x $5,000 = $ 200,000 Land Cost

320 spaces x $2,500 = 800,000 Development Cost

$1,000,000 Total Cost

Interest on construction loan is:

$$\frac{4\% \times \$800,000}{2} \; + \; (4\% \times \$800,000) \qquad = \; \$\ 48,000$$

Rent Income for 2 Years is:

First Year

$$12 \times \frac{(180 \text{ spaces} \times \$60)}{2} \qquad = \; \$\ 64,800$$

Second Year

$$12 \left[\frac{(180 \text{ spaces} \times \$60)}{2} + (180 \text{ spaces} \times \$60]) \right] \; = \; \$194,400$$

Total $259,200

To Determine Capital Needed:

Equity Capital is $1,000,000 less

$800,000 Loan $200,000

Add

Working Capital 20,000

Contingencies 20,000

Construction Loan Interest 48,000

1½ Year Long Term

Mortgage Payment 119,520

Operating Cost for 2 Years 148,000

Loan Fee 16,000

Total $571,520

Deduct

Income for First Two Years 259,200

Capital Needed $322,320

It is true that many parks are filled long before a two year period, especially if a prime site is found. Sometimes parks in prime locations are completely rented even before construction is completed. On the other hand, to invest savings on the assumption that this is a typical situation is imprudent. The wise investor will approach the park industry with the same prudence that he approaches any other industry. He will do so conservatively, being sure that he has sufficient capital to carry him through possible difficulties so that he will not be risking loss of all that he has invested. The example given above is meant only for quick analysis of an investment. Before becoming firmly committed, your accountant should prepare a monthly cash flow chart.

Financing

Another success factor is the matter of financing. Two types of financing are required in the construction of a park. A construction loan and a take out long term mortgage loan is required. The degree of difficulty in obtaining these loans will depend upon the money market at the time the park is to be constructed; it will depend too, on the financial stability of the principles involved in the development of the park.

Zoning

A major problem for a park developer is frequently the matter of obtaining proper zoning. Once a desirable piece of property is located, it may be necessary to obtain zoning which will permit the construction of a park. Ordinarily, if the land is within city limits, zoning is more difficult to obtain than if it is in the county area.

Local Laws

Another matter deserving careful attention in planning the development of a park is the local codes relating to the development of a park. Many communities have now enacted laws which regulate all aspects of recreational vehicle and mobile home park construction and operation. These laws must be reviewed with careful attention to their relevance to cost factors, both in construction and operation.

Management

Management is always a critical factor in park operation. There are so many dimensions to management that only those who have had proper training and/or experience can successfully cope with the many difficulties which must be overcome by the park manager.

Professional Help

Another area deserving careful attention is the competent advice which is necessary during both the construction and operation of a park. To any industry which is booming there flock those who represent themselves as highly qualified to be retained as consultants. We have already discussed procedures for avoiding the retention of those who might not be properly qualified.

Cost Vs. Income

Finally, let us consider the intricacies of evaluating cost factors versus income factors in determining whether to invest in a mobile home park. Costs are variable and income is variable. The questions of how much to invest and how much income can be expected are highly technical but crucial questions. Obviously the amount which can successfully be invested is related to the amount of income which can reasonably be anticipated. To go by so called industry rules-of-thumb is to invite disaster. To say that no more than $2000 per space should be invested in a mobile home park or no more than $500 per space in a recreational vehicle park, to say that no more than $1,000 an acre should be paid for recreational vehicle park land or no more than $5,000 an acre for mobile home park land is to overlook the real investment opportunities which exist in the park industry. The fact is that the amount which can be invested is directly related to the amount of income which can be realized. To mention an extreme example there is not a single reason why land cannot be purchased at $100,000 an acre and $5,000 per space be put into development costs, provided the location and the plant are sufficient to warrant a rental rate which will adequately reward this type of investment. I can personally attest to a feasability study prepared by Park Management Associates under my supervision which will soon result in a ten acre Recreational Vehicle Park on leased land worth $130,000 per acre; the study projects a 95% cash flow to investors. This means the amount of equity capital invested will be returned almost 100% to the investors each year! Those who are investigating the park industry would be well-advised not to put their minds in the strait-jackets of industry averages. The correct frame of mind is to compare income to costs and make the investment based upon a proper evaluation of those factors.

STEPS TO A PROFITABLE PARK INVESTMENT

The first question the prospective investor in the park industry should ask is "What steps must I take in order to be a successful park investor and how long does it take?"

It takes from six months to three and one-half years, depending on factors we will explain later.

This chapter is devoted to answering the balance of the question. The steps are as follows:

1. The first step is making a decision of whether to invest in the park industry or to invest elsewhere. This step can be time consuming for one who is just learning about the industry and wants to thoroughly investigate it before making a decision. For others who are acquainted with the industry and know its opportunities, or for those who rely upon investment counselors who have such knowledge, the decision can be almost immediate.

2. Having decided to invest, you next decide on the form of business organization that is to be used for the new park. You must decide whether the park should be owned by an individual proprietorship, by a partnership, by a limited partnership, or by a corporation. Each form of ownership has its advantages and disadvantages. To a large extent, the form of organization will depend on the personal position of those who are investing and upon tax and legal considerations. Advice in this area should naturally be obtained from your attorney and your tax counselor. This step should not be too time consuming.

3. Decide how much you can invest. This, of course, relates to your personal wealth and the amount of risk you wish to take in this particular industry.

Should you have insufficient capital, there is the matter of persuading others to join in the venture. Of course, when others must be attracted to obtain the necessary capital, considerable time may be required to get through this step.

4. Locate the area in which the proposed park is to be placed. In this step the investor must make a preliminary area feasibility study to determine whether the area is in need of a park. This step need not be very time consuming and will be discussed in full in a later chapter.

5. Having selected a desirable area the next step is to to find a suitable parcel of land. This can be a time consuming step and it will discussed in full in a later chapter.

6. Conduct a preliminary site feasibility study. This need take only a day or two and again, we shall discuss this in detail in a later chapter.

7. Obtain an option on the land that is to be purchased for the park. In states where real estate transactions are handled through escrows, an escrow is opened, with the buyer and seller giving their instruction to the escrow agent. From the buyer's point of view the option must be conditional upon such factors as:

   A. Ability to obtain zoning.

   B. Ability of seller to provide clear title and a title insurance policy in states where these are available.

   C. Buyer's written acceptance of terms, conditions, and covenants, as they may be discovered in the title papers pertaining to the parcel of land being purchased.

   D. Buyer's ability to obtain necessary mortgage financing.

   E. If Seller has made any representations that are material to the successful development of a park, the buyer should have the right to terminate the option should it develop that any of these representations are false. Such representation should be clearly stated in the escrow papers.

In states where escrows are not the conventional manner for handling real estate transactions, these matters can be handled by contract, using means accepted in that state. Such an option usually carries a time limit of six months to one year, depending upon the complexity of the circumstances and the amount of effort which buyer must put forth before he can be sure that he can go ahead with the project.

8. Prepare a feasibility study. This should be professionally prepared and will be a requirement at the time mortgage financing is sought. Reputable professional help should be obtained for this purpose. The amount of time required is normally from three to four weeks. Additional time may be required if data required for such a study is not readily available. If the preliminary data collected in a feasibility study indicates a favorable investment, then preliminary engineering should become part of the feasibility study stage of the development. Preliminary engineering provides a layout for the park, preliminary building design, and preliminary costs. When these elements are available, the feasibility study can be completed to show the economic factors which ultimately determine the feasibility of the project.

9. The next step is to obtain zoning. In many cases zoning will readily be available for the site; in fact, the land is sometimes already zoned to allow a park. Sometimes a zoning variance or conditional use permit must be obtained from zoning officials. This step can be fast or considerably time consuming, depending upon the conditions in the local community. There are regular legal procedures which must be followed if you are seeking a variance or a conditional use permit. The feasibility study prepared in the previous step will already indicate whether or not zoning is likely to be easy or difficult. Should zoning appear to be a difficult hurdle, it is wise to seek professional advice. A great deal may be at

stake in a zoning hearing. Proper presentation is essential if you want to maximize your chances of succeeding. We will not discuss in detail the many facets of zoning in this book. There have been many books written on this subject.

A brief discussion of suggestions for success in a zoning hearing does belong in this book, however. A park zoning hearing is a public hearing at which a park developer seeks to obtain zoning which permits him to build and operate a park on a specific parcel of land. In such a meeting the developer presents his case and then those who oppose the development may speak. This is followed by a period during which the developer may counter arguments presented by opponents of the park.

The developer must be prepared to *sell* mobile home living as a benefit to the community, and he be prepared to refute the typical arguments opponents will present. To this end the following suggestions are made:

1. Present a plot plan, preliminary drawings of structures and a layout of a typical mobile home site. Back this up with colored architectural renderings to demonstrate the quality of the development and its compatibility with and contribution to the community. Emphasize recreation facilities planned.

2. Be prepared to show how the development will be far superior to any substandard park developments in the area.

3. Show color slides and/or movies of attractive mobile home parks *and* of deluxe mobile home exteriors and interiors.

4. Include slides which demonstrate the dominant role modern mobile home housing is playing in solving the nation's low and medium price housing needs. These are available from the national associations.

5. Demonstrate the need for spaces by presenting surveys of vacancy factors in present parks and

mobile home dealer statements concerning the need.

6. Relate the park to the master plan for the community, showing how it is compatible with that plan.

7. Present financial data to demonstrate the developer's stability and ability to follow through.

8. Present statistics on the anticipated number of school children who will live in the park, as compared to such figures for conventional housing.

9. Present data which will demonstrate what revenue the community can expect, compared to costs the community will experience as a result of the park.

10. Have expert witnesses available who can testify concerning:

   A. The effect of a park on surrounding property values.

   B. The amount of tax revenue the park will generate and its costs to the community as contrasted to conventional housing.

   C. The types of residents attracted to mobile home living.

10. Line up both construction and long-term mortgage financing. This step is usually quite time consuming. If loan money is plentiful, you will want to shop for the best rate of interest; if loan money is scarce, it may require considerable shopping to obtain a loan which is consistent with the return you expect, as outlined by the feasibility study. This matter will be discussed in a later chapter.

11. The next step is to employ an achitect to do the engineering. Professional help is required, of course. It is to your advantage to obtain assistance from architects with experience in the park field, if this is possible.

12. Prepare the final plot plan. At this time, a complete set of working drawings and specifications is prepared by the architect.

13. Obtain bids on the project.
14. Let the bid to a competent, reliable general contractor. He may not necessarily be the low bidder. Completion bonds should be required. The reputation of the contractor in the community is of prime importance. A contractor who has done park work before may be preferable.
15. Obtain permits, both city, county, and state, for construction of the park.
16. The general contractor will begin with rough grading of the site, including the rough grading for roads.
17. He will then subcontract work which results in the water, sewer, phones, TV lines, and gas lines being put into the park.
18. He will then complete grading for lots and buildings.
19. Now he contracts work required for putting in buildings, setting up the sites, and putting in the necessary paving.
20. Final grading and landscaping.
21. Final projects such as cleanup, mail boxes, clothes lines, etc.
22. The next step, which is somewhat out of chronological order since this step should be taken approximately three months before the park is to open, is to hire management for the park.
23. Begin promotion of the park. This too should precede completion of the park, since it will be possible to rent spaces before the park is completed.
24. Fill park with residents.
25. Keep the park filled with residents through the use of proven management techniques.

We began this chapter with the statement that it could take from six months to three and one-half years from the point of decision to a filled park earning an excellent return. This span of time will be dependent upon many, many factors. The steps themselves have been detailed above, but let me speak from personal experience in giving you a little more insight into the time factor. I have known of parks which have been built and filled in six months (or slightly less) from the time when a decision was made. Obviously, such a park was built in an area where spaces were scarce and there was a heavy demand. The park was filled before it was completed. There was no zoning problem, contracting problem, capital or loan problem, and experienced park architects and contractors were used. A problem with any one of these factors will mean delay; the delay is lengthened if problems compound. At this time is would be fair to say that the average park takes approximately two years from the time the decision to build is made to the time when the park is full.

INCOME POTENTIAL

One of the most frequently asked questions by an investor who is investigating the park industry is, "What rate of return can I get on my investment?"

Those who ask such a question are usually looking for a specific answer, such as ten, 15, or 20 percent. It is our purpose in this chapter to realistically discuss the answer to this question. First, however, it should be recognized that there is no simple answer to this question. The correct answer to the question is "it depends upon many factors." We have already pointed out that the keys to success in the park industry are location, plant, and management. A park built in a well-chosen location, properly constructed with facilities suited to that location, and well-managed, will reward the investor with an excellent return, perhaps an investment return better than that available from just about any other segment of the American economy.

But to use this fact to justify the assumption that any park is a good investment would be a mistake. I have heard some experts in the industry state, unequivocably, that there are no unsuccessful parks. In a sense, this may be true. The demand for park spaces is so strong that eventually any park that is built will probably fill. The question becomes one of how soon it will fill, and do the original investors have sufficient reserves to hold onto the park in the interim. Although most parks are successful in the sense that they are eventually built and filled and offer a good return to the investors, the investors who ultimately own the park may be a different group than those who started the project. Such a change in ownership takes places when the original investors are undercapitalized so that they are not able to hold the park until it becomes a profitable operation.

Pitfall of Over-optimism

There are many connected with the park industry who geninunely believe that an unsuccessful park is almost impossible. In their zeal to increase the number of spaces available for mobile homes and recreational vehicles (a need which is unquestioned), association executives, mobile home manufacturers, recreational vehicle manufacturers, contractors, architects, franchisers, and realtors, at times, are overly optimistic concrning a park at any given location and therefore fail to carefully make a detailed investment analysis of the project.

It should be made clear at this point that in this chapter I am relying upon personal experience. The data which is being presented is naturally colored by this experience. My personal experience in the park industry is based on hundreds of consulting sessions with park developers and owners, the preparation of many feasibility studies connected with new park construction, direct involvement in the management of numerous parks in which the firm with whom I am associated (Park Management Associates) has property management contracts, and reviewing hundreds of balance sheets and income statements for parks throughout the United States. In conection with consulting sessions and management, it would be fair to say that a management firm frequently is called into park situations where difficulties are being experienced; for that reason, my evaluation may be colored by an overabundance of problem situations. All of the problems we have been called upon to deal with fall under the three headings: location, plant, or management. It is almost impossible to correct location problems; problems relating to plant can be solved only by the expenditure of considerable sums of money, whereas problems relating to management are usually quickly solved by application of correct management techniques.

Rules Of Thumb

The typical investor is usually seeking rules of thumb by which he can evaluate a proposed investment. He wants to know, for example, what percentage of gross income goes to expenses, how much per acre he can afford to pay for land, how much per space he can spend for development, his rate of cash flow, his rate of equity buildup, what depreciation rates can be used, and what type of tax shelter the park industry offers. We are now going to discuss some of these matters in detail. First, however, we would like to again emphasize that rules of thumb are not a satisfactory basis for evaluating a park investment. The only safe procedure is to take a specific location and evaluate all of the factors relating to that location.

Park Income

Let us first look at how parks generate income. The determining factors in the level of income are: location, quality of plant, quality of management, and competition. On a nationwide basis rents vary from as little as $25 per month to $300 and up. Those parks which enjoy a high level of rental rates are obviously well located, deluxe in features, and well managed.

Let us now look at each source of income.

1. Space rents. Eighty-five to 95 percent of a park's gross income is realized through space rents. This is true of both the mobile home park and the recreational vehicle park. In recreational vehicle parks, there may be other income-generating operations associated with the park such as stores; but these should really be considered separate operations.

2. Guest Charges. When guests visit a park for a protracted period of time it is assumed that it will put an extra burden on park services; charges are therefore usually made for guests who are in the park for more than a few days (provides 0 to 1% of gross income).

3. Extra Persons Income. Most parks base their rents on the theory that the average family is three persons. Additional charges are often made for additional family members to cover costs which the park must bear as a result of having additional persons using its facilities (provides 0 to 1% of gross income).

4. Pet Charges. Many parks permit pets on a restricted basis and make an extra charge for this privilege

(proivdes 0 to 2% of gross income).

5. Storage of Recreational Vehicles. Mobile home parks frequently have a section set aside for the storage of recreational vehicles. 20 to 25 percent of the nation's mobile home owners own a recreational vehicle of one type of another. It is not desirable, for aesthetic reasons, to permit recreational vehicles to be parked on the mobile home lot. Fees are often charged for a storage space in a recreational vehicle storage area (provides 0 to 1% of gross income).

6. Natural Gas. Possibility of income to the park for the sale of natural gas depends upon the policies set up by the gas company and public utility commission regulating the community where the park is located. In some cases, the gas company insists upon metering the gas directly to the resident and billing the resident. In such a case there is no profit opportunity for the park. In other cases, the utility company provides a master gas meter but does not meter the gas to each space. The park pays the utility company on the basis of total gas used and recovers some or all this cost by charging the resident, using a flat monthly charge for gas or a billing formula based on the number of square feet in his mobile home, the rates varying with the season. In other cases the park puts in meters to each space, reads those meters and bills the resident at a profit to the park. In recreational vehicle parks, gas income is realized by the sale of liquefied petroleum gas to those who need their tanks refilled (provides 0 to 3% of gross income).

7. Sale of Oil. In some areas the principal source of fuel for heating is oil. Parks can install a central oil distribution system to service the mobile homes in the park and realize a profit from the sale of oil to the residents (provides 0 to 2% of gross income).

8. Sale of Power. Many mobile home parks generate income from the sale of power to residents. It purchases power from the utility company on a demand

meter basis and resells it on a metered basis to each of the residents at a markup. This is possible only when permitted by the Public Utility Commission and the power company. In recreational vehicle parks this item is usually considered as included in the rental rate (provides 0 to 3% of park income).

9. Water Sales. In almost all cases the amount of water used by a mobile home resident is included in his basic rental rate. This is true for a recreational vehicle park too. In a few exceptional cases the resident is asked to pay a flat monthly water fee in addition to his rent.

10. The modern mobile home park installs a central TV antenna system to eliminate an unsightly forest of TV antennas. The resident is required to pay a monthly fee for connection to the system. This generates a profit for the park (provides 0 to 2.5% of gross income).

11. Laundry Service. Both mobile home parks and recreational vehicle parks generate substantial income from laundry service. Service buildings are established containing coin operated washers and dryers. Income from this source represents a substantially higher percentage of gross income in a recreational vehicle park (provides 2 to 15% of gross income).

12. Coin Machines. The installation of coin machines in a mobile home park is to some extent a service to residents, but it does generate a small amount of income. In a recreational vehicle park coin machines can generate a substantial amount of income (provides 0 to 2% of gross income).

Even if it were possible to break total income down into percentage categories by making a national survey of thousands of parks, this would be of very little value to a potential investor. What is important is what income can be derived from each type of service *in the area where that particular park is going to be developed*. To use rules of thumb can easily lead to an unsound investment.

Park Expenses

Let us now turn our attention to the cost factors in a mobile home or recreational vehicle park. They are as follows:

Management

Each park requires management. This is usually a man and wife team. (Runs 5 to 15% of gross income.)

Extra Personnel

Larger parks also require maintenance personnel. One or more employees may be needed. In large parks, where recreation program are a special feature, a recreation director is sometimes employed. (Runs 0 to 5% of gross income.)

Payroll Taxes

Since salaries are paid to management and other employees, payroll taxes are a cost factor. (Runs .5 to 2% of gross income.)

Utilities

Parks have expenses connected with the use of gas and power. When the park is able to meter and bill these items directly to the tenants, its cost in this connection usually disappears; it can even realize a profit. Water is an expense which may be small or large, depending upon the source of water. Water that must be obtained from wells can become a substantial expense due to the cost of maintaining the pumping and storage facilities. (Runs 0 to 4% of gross income.)

Sewers

Sewers may be a small or a large expense. If public sewers are available, expense is usually minor. Usually a monthly charge for each space is collected by the local political unit having jurisdiction over sewers. If public sewers are not available, then a sewage treatment plant or septic tank system must be provided; expense for sewage disposal then becomes a substantial park of park income. (Runs 1 to 5% of gross income.)

Insurance

Insurance expense in parks is usually a very minor item. Insurance must be purchased to cover compensation insurance for employees. The park itself must be protected with public liability insurance and fire insurance with extended coverage. (Runs .5 to 1% of gross income.)

Property Tax

This can represent a minor or major expense, depending upon the area where the park is located. (Runs 1 to 15% of gross income.)

Licenses

Both a business license and a license to operate a park must usually be purchased. These are very minor items. (Runs .1 to .25% of gross income.)

Maintenance

Costs here vary widely, depending on the quality of the park and its geographical location. It is usually a major expense item. (Runs 5 to 10% of gross income.)

Advertising

This is a substantial expense item when a park is new and ownership is advertising heavily to fill the park. Once the park is filled it becomes a very minor expense. (Runs .1 to 2% of gross income.)

Dues and Subscriptions

This is always a minor expense, covering such things as association dues and magazines for the park recreation room. (Runs .1 to .8% of gross income.)

Legal

An investment in a park may require legal services from time to time, but this is a minor expense in the long run. (Runs 0 to .5% of gross income.)

Accounting

Most parks employ a CPA to oversee accounting operation and prepare tax forms. This is usually a minimal expense. (Runs 0 to 1% of gross income.)

Auto and Mechanical

The number of vehicles a park owns depends upon the size of the park. The park may have a truck for hauling trash and handling gardening chores; it may have a station wagon or other automobile available to the management; and it may have snow removal equipment in the cold climates. This is a highly variable expense item depending upon the location and nature of the park. (Runs from 0 to

4% of gross income.)

Office Expense

This expense is usually minimal. (Runs from .2 to 1% of gross income.)

Telephone

This is also a minimal expense. (Runs from .1 to .5% of gross income.)

Trash

This will usually represent a cost of moderate proportion. Trash removal is either handled on a contract basis or by the park itself. (Runs 2 to 4% of gross income.)

Land Rent

If the park is located on leased land, this will probably be the largest expense on the income statement. (Runs 20 to 50% of gross income.)

Laundry Expense

Just about all parks provide laundry facilities on a coin operated basis, but there are a few minor expenses connected with this service. Sometimes soap is supplied free as well as water softeners. There is usually a special water heater which services these laundry facilities. This, too, is a minimal expense item. (Runs .5 to 3% of gross income.)

Travel

This expense may be large or small, depending upon the location of the principals who own the park and the frequency of their desire to visit it. (Runs 0 to 1.5% of gross income.)

Entertainment

Most parks provide some funds to entertain residents at annual parties, such as Christmas, Thanksgiving, or other occasions. Coffee and doughnuts are frequently provided year-round in the recreation room at the park's expense. In most parks this a minor expense. In deluxe parks it may be a substantial cost item. (Runs .2 to 1.5% of gross income.)

Miscellaneous

This is a catchall for minor expenses that defy categorization. The amount is always small. (Runs 1 to 3% of gross income.)

Total Costs as Percent of Income

The above items are the normal expense items that

appear in a park income statement as a cost of operation (There are other "non-operating" costs such as depreciation and interest; they are better considered apart from normal operating costs, however.) What percentage of total income (excluding interest and depreciation) should normal costs represent? Are total costs 50 percent of income? Are they 20 percent of income? Or do they lie somewhere between these two extremes? The answer depends upon the particular situation. A few general statements can be made in this connection.

1. Total operating costs can be much more than 50 percent of income in periods when the park is filling.
2. Parks in areas where high rental rates can be realized usually enjoy a lower percentage of operating cost.
3. The larger the park the lower will be the percentage of operating costs.

On a national average, operating costs in parks which are 95 percent full or more, vary somewhere between 45 percent and 28 percent of gross revenues. The larger parks as well as those having high rental rates enjoy the lower percentage rates. In analyzing any particular investment, it is necessary to look at the specific costs connected with the operation of that particular location to determine what actual ratio of cost to income will develop.

Depreciation

Let us now turn our attention to depreciation. This may or may not be a substantial part of park overall costs. The Internal Revenue Service has established no guidelines for depreciation rates for mobile home or recreational vehicle parks. Structures on conventional real estate are usually depreciated at a 40 year rate. When all of the costs of developing a mobile home park are recorded in an account designated as "land improvements", the developer or investor has considerable latitude in selecting the period of time over which he will depreciate his park. On a national average knowledgeable park operators charge off park investments over a 15 to 20 year period. The usual accelerated depreciation methods are available to park owners. The best depreciation rate is a matter for determination by conference with the owner's tax consultants, however. The usual justification for depreciating parks on a basis of less than 40 years is two-fold. First, mobile home and recreational vehicle parks are usually interim land use; the history of the industry has been that land values have increased to such an extent that a park soon finds itself on land of such value that it is more desirable to level the park and put the land to other use. Second, there has been a high factor of obsolesence in the park field due to technological changes which have taken place in the industry.

Interest

Interest is a financial expense that can be a substantial factor in overall costs. When there is a substantial loan on a park, the mortgage payment absorbs a substantial amount of the income flow. This payment consists of two elements. One is the interest on the mortgage; the other is payment on principal. As the principal is paid, there is an increase in equity which the owners enjoy as a result of paying off the mortgage. Interest on the mortgage is a deductible expense. Developers and invevstors frequently prefer a maximum loan for the purpose of obtaining maximum leverage on their invested capital.

Measuring Rate of Return

There are three factors which must be evaluated to measure the total amount of return to the investor.

1. The amount of the cash available to the investor after payment of mortgage and all park expenses. This is cash available for distribution to owners; it's usually referred to as "cash flow". It is not unusual to see the annual cash flow percentage for a properly located, well built and professionally managed park at somewhere between 15 percent and 35 percent of the actual amount of invested capital as represented by the equity investment of investors. In unusual situations this rate of return can be considerably higher.

2. The second return to the investor is the increase in his equity in the park as the cash generated by the park liquidates the principal of the loan.

3. A third factor benefiting the investor is the tax shelter provided by depreciation. When parks are depreciated over a 15 to 20 year period, using various accelerated depreciation methods, income may be sheltered from income tax for a period of four to seven years, depending upon the partcular circumstances.

Due to the many variables and the inability to specifically pin down both expenses and income to rules of thumb, it is obvious that a proposed investment must be evaluated based upon the circumstances which will apply to that particular investment. In making investment analysis, the correct procedure is to prepare pro forma income statements for the first three years of operation. In doing so, a realistic evaluation must be made of the projected flow of income from the park, and a specific analysis must be made of each expense item relating to that park. One of the functions of the feasibility study is to provide this type of pro forma statement.

Investment Mistakes

Let us conclude this chapter on income potential by detailing some of the mistakes investors have made in the past so that those who are currently investigating the industry can avoid these misfortunes.

1. Far too frequently park investments have been undertaken with inadequate capitalization. The result of such a situation is that the park must be sold to other investors who can finish the construction or await the filling of the park. In such situations, original investors usually are forced to sell their interest at a substantial loss. Very careful analysis of required capitalization should always be made with ample safety factors built-in to prevent this situation.

2. Some have sought to circumvent the use of qualified architects and contractors. This can result in two difficulties for an investor. One is poor design of the park; this results in a plant which is not built to handle the market, or one which is expensive to

maintain. The second difficulty that arises is an excess cost of construction which, of course, increases capital requirements.

3. Parks have frequently been undertaken without the preparation of proper feasibility studies. Such parks are often franchise operations, real estate promotions, and proposals made by those who are anxious to see spaces built for the industry. The "feasability studies" prepared have far too optimistic a rent projection; construction costs are often far below realistic levels; no consideration is given to the cost of construction loan interest, or to a number of points related to obtaining mortgage money; operating costs are under-estimated; no provision is made for working capital; there is no safety factor built into capital requirements to cover necessary expenditures while the park is being filled or to cover unforeseen expenses.

4. Parks are sometimes over-built for the market they are seeking to capture. This can be avoided only by a realistic evaluation of the amount of rent that can be obtained, followed by building the park with features consistent with that level of income.

5. Substantial amounts of money are often invested in preliminary work on a park only to discover that both mortgage loans and zoning are difficult, if not completely unobtainable.

6. Management is often a critical problem. The investor frequently feels that anyone can operate a mobile home or recreational vehicle park and that the untrained person can quickly pick up the required techniques. Mobile home and recreational vehicle park management is often compared to apartment or motel management where extensive training or experience is not required. Investors often seek to set management salaries low, forgetting that their park invevstment is substantial and that it should be protected by highly competent management personnel. As we shall see in the chapter dealing with management, the management of either a mobile home or

recreational vehicle park is a highly specialized skill. Management is one of the three keys to success; the best located and best built plant, can suffer numerous problems and fail to realize potential income if adequate management is not provided. Such management can be obtained by employing those who have demonstrated proficiency in the industry through experience, by employing those who have had adequate training, or by entering into property management contracts with firms who are qualified to operate parks.

7. Far too often an overly optimistic projection is made for the period of time in which the park will fill. It is often assumed that a park will fill almost immediately, that it will fill within six months, or even a year. An informed and realistic evaluation would lead to an entirely different conclusion in many cases. Overly optimistic projections for filling the park result in overly optimistic income flow and failure to provide adequate capital reserves.

8. Investors seeking to enter the industry often prefer to buy an existing park rather than to accept the period of time required to develop a new park. The purchase of an existing park should be very carefully evaluated. Parks that are successful and have an excellent income flow are for sale at premium rates. Parks having difficulties, for one reason or another, may be available for sale, but the price may be no bargain. I would advise the average investor to develop a new park as contrasted with purchasing one already built. He is much more likely to enjoy an attractive return.

9. Recreational vehicle parks are often rejected as an investment because too low a rental rate is used for projections. Recreational vehicle parks with excellent facilities do not need to be restricted to rental rates close to those offered in public facilities. A large segment of the public wants excellent facilities and will pay prices commensurate with the facilities offered.

10. There are an increasing number of firms which offer Park Franchises. Such francises should be bought only after the most thorough investigation. Recent Federal Trade Commission hearings revealed many interesting facts concerning the rapidly growing Franchising Business. No doubt legislation will result in an effort to "clean up" some of the objectional practices in the franchise industry.

The wise developer interested in a franchise will:

1. Deal with a franchisor who is financially strong so that if it develops that he does not receive all he has been sold he will have an opportunity to recover his investment.

2. Thoroughly check the reputation of the franchisor.

3. Be sure that all services promised him are specifically detailed in writing in the franchise contract.

4. Verify that the franchisor does indeed have industry know-how by checking with others who have operating franchises to determine their experiences.

5. Verify that fees paid the franchisor are reasonable and leave the operator a fair return for his labor and investment.

A recreational vehicle park franchise can have merit if the seller is reputable and provides know-how, national advertising, management assistance and a cooperative reservation system, and if franchise fees are reasonable.

I seriously question the value of some mobile home park franchises, however. National advertising and reservations are of little or no value because residents are permanent. Industry know how and management guidance can be purchased from industry professionals for flat fees without having a permanent drain on park income in the form of a percent of income as a franchise fee. If the franchise is a joint venture, with both the franchisor and franchisee sharing in providing equity capital, then a mobile home park franchise may be desirable.

SITE LOCATION

Once a decision has been made to invest in a park, the obvious first step is to locate a site. This chapter will suggest a procedure to be used for proper site selection. The procedure can be broken into three phases. *Phase one* is to study a large area to locate a community in which a park is needed. *Phase two* is to locate a specific parcel of land in this community. *The third phase* is to make a detailed feasibility study of this parcel to determine its investment potential as a mobile home or recreational vehicle park.

Area Study

Let us first turn our attention to phase 1. Specifically what steps should be taken to determine whether a given community is a desirable site for park investment. For practical purposes limit the "community" to a five mile radius. You are more likely to succeed in locating a desirable community if you start with communities where mobile home living is established. A preliminary survey of the community to determine its adaptability to a successful park would include the following.

1. Large dealers in the community should be visited. Inquiries should be made concerning the need for additional parks, what type of park is desirable, and how long they think such a new park would take to fill.
2. Visit parks in the community which might be competitive to anticipated facilities. Notations should be made of the type of residents, number of spaces, quality and age of the park, rental rates, extra charges, and vacancy rates.
3. Contact the local planning board to determine the difficulty of obtaining zoning for parks in that community.

4. Contact the building department to determine what parks are underway in the community, and what parks are in planning stages, so that you can evaluate potential new competition.

5. Inquiries should be made of financial institutions in the community to determine what financing is possible.

6. If there is a trade association representing the mobile home and/or recreational vehicle industry in the community, obtain information concerning their knowledge of the need for parks.

7. The local chamber of commerce should be visited. It should be helpful in determining the community's attitude toward parks. Possibly it can help evaluate the need for a park.

8. Visit real estate agents in the community. They are in a good position to know how many people are shopping for park land in the community. They often have information concerning the need.

9. If a recreational vehicle park is contemplated, several additional steps should be taken. The chamber of commerce should be contacted regarding the number of Recreational Vehicle owners who inquire about spaces. Mobile home parks that take overnighters should be visited to determine their vacancy rates, their rental rates, and seasonal vacancy data should also be obtained. Recreational vehicle dealers should be visited, as should recreational vehicle parks in the community. Service stations are frequently also helpful since travelers stop at service stations to ask where spaces may be available. Visit the service stations at major highway intersections and determine from them how many space inquiries they receive.

Preliminary Site Survey

When an area preliminary feasibility survey has located a community in need of a park, the second step is to locate land which is suitable for the park. In this connection, a preliminary land study should be made for each piece of land being considered. It should reflect data concerning the following:

1. Cost of the land.
2. Size of the parcel.
3. Terrain. Land which is hilly may require considerable grading; this is an expensive procedure. Land with a slight slope is the most desirable.
4. Soil condition. This is especially important if a septic tank system must be established. It can also seriously affect construction cost.
5. Flood control must be considered. A parcel which otherwise might be acceptable could be ruled out because of flood control problems that might necessitate the expenditures of substantial sums of money.
6. Negative factors such as noise or objectionable odors should be considered. Land near an airport, industrial area, or farm area should receive especially careful evaluation in this regard.
7. Accessibility is another consideration. This is especially true of the recreational vehicle park since it needs to be close to main highways and major attractions. Mobile home parks may be off the beaten path, provided there is access to the park.
8. Shopping facilities should be nearby.
9. If the park is to be one of which accepts families and working people, then employment should be nearby.
10. Parks which will accept children should be close to schools.
11. Public transportation not too far away is, of course, always desirable.
12. The availability of water, sewer, power, gas, phone, and TV reception are matters deserving very careful attention. Sometimes excessively high costs of bringing any one of the major utilities to a site will be sufficient to eliminate that site as a possible park.
13. Is favorable zoning possible? The land may already be zoned to permit a park. Often, however, a zone change or conditional use permit must be obtained.

Should this be difficult to obtain, the land may have to be rejected for this reason alone.

Feasibility Study

If a preliminary area survey and a preliminary land survey result in your optioning a parcel of land, a feasibility study is your next step. A feasibility study is an extremely important step toward your investment goal. Professionals with wide knowledge of the mobile home and recreational vehicle park industry should be consulted. Care in selecting the individual or firm to conduct the study is most important. No firm or individual should conduct the study who might have a future financial gain to make from the study; the whole purpose of the study is lost if impartiality is sacrificed. Such a study may most advantageously be conducted in four phases for the purpose of eliminating unnecessary expense.

The first phase should be a conference with a firm of good reputation and knowledge in the industry. At this conference you pass on to that firm the information you have collected regarding the area and the parcel of land. At this stage, if you are advised that the parcel does not appear to be satisfactory for good reasons, the study should be dropped. If you and a counseling firm decide that the site appears favorable, then you should proceed with the second phase of the study.

The second phase involves detailed study of the economic factors in the community that will affect the investment. It should also include a detailed study of all factors which relate to the land parcel selected.

Phase two should result in a written detailed report answering the following questions:

1. What present and potential competition exists for the proposed park?
2. What rental rates are being charged by parks in the community?
3. Is the terrain satisfactory for a park?
4. Are there drawbacks, such as noise, odors, inharmonious neighborhood, or land maintenance factors (excessive winds, dust, etc.)?

5. What are the occupancy rates for established parks in the community?

6. Are there flood conditions relating to the selected piece of property? If any exist, what is the cost of correcting them?

7. What is the condition of the soil for the proposed site?

8. What factors are there in the community that will influence the park's success? An analysis should be made of the community's growth, the amount of of employment offered in the community, housing conditions and the community's attitude toward the proposed park.

9. What facilities, such as playgrounds, swimming pool, recreation building, and utility rooms should the park offer?

10. What quality should be built into the park? Should costs be kept to a minimum or should substantial funds be invested to build the finest park in the community?

11. What laws will affect the development of the park? State, county, and city laws should be thoroughly investigated and reported.

12. What is the situation regarding available utilities? Are gas, power, water, sewer, and TV facilities readily available? If not, what will it cost to make them available?

13. What is the reaction of dealers in the community to the proposed park?

14. What is the attitude of the community concerning the proposed park?

15. What probability is there of obtaining zoning?

16. Is the land value stated in the option a fair price? What are the chances of appreciation?

17. What type of park should be built? Should it be a retirement park, a second home park, an all adult park, a family park, a working man's park, or perhaps a combination?

18. What size should the spaces be?

19. What architects and contractors are available in the

community who are qualified to design and build the park?

20. What taxes will be paid by the new park?
21. What license fees will be required?
22. What unusual cost factors may be involved in the construction of the park?
23. If public sewers are not available, what type of sewage system should be built? Is there enough land for a septic tank and drainage field? How much will a sewage treatment plant cost?

When this written report has been submitted, the investor will have adequate data to determine whether he should proceed further. If the decision is to proceed, the third phase of a feasibility study may be undertaken.

The third phase of a feasibility study (preliminary engineering) requires the employment of a park architect, preferably one with considerable experience, and with a highly regarded reputation in the park industry. The park architect will require a topographic map, a boundary survey of the property, and information regarding easements. He can then prepare a plot plan and preliminary plans for engineering. He can also prepare a cost breakdown, showing all costs of developing the proposed park. The architect should have a copy of the feasibility study developed in phase 2. This will alert him to special difficulties requiring close attention. He needs to know the accessibility of water, sewer, gas, and utilities; he needs information on terrain, soil, local building codes, etc. It must be emphasized that phase three involves only *preliminary* engineering. Detailed and costly final engineering should not be undertaken until phase four shows the park is a good investment.

Phase 4 of the feasibility study investigates the economics of park operation to determine whether the investment is wise. The report will show the total amount of investment which must be made, the amount which may be borrowed, and the amount of equity capital which must be offered by the investors. It will provide a projected three year operating statement for the park, showing the amount of the gain or loss at the end of each of the first three years of operation. It will relate costs of operation to potential income flow, taking into consideration mortgage payments, construction loan interest, working capital, and contingency funds. Loan amortization, depreciation, and income tax tables will be provided, and a percentage rate will be established for both spendable cash flow as its relates to equity capital and equity buildup. This final phase of the feasibility study is the culmination of the study inasmuch as it brings all three of the preceding phases to bear on the question "is the park a wise investment?" Obviously, no intelligent decision can be made until the fourth phase is complete.

To specifically illustrate the feasibility study procedure we have included in the appendix an actual sample of parts of a study together with informative comments.

DESIGN AND ENGINEERING

As I have advised previously, the only sensible approach to obtaining proper design and engineering is to use professionals with experience and high reputation in the park industry. The introduction tells you how to obtain such personnel.

The feasibility study provides preliminary design in phase 3. Included is a plot plan showing the number of spaces, roads, and buildings. This preliminary engineering is now subject to considerable scrutiny and possible revision. Consider now the factors which bear on preparing final design and engineering.

Grading. Grading should be kept to a minimum. Natural drainage channels should be used, where possible. Advantage should be taken of all natural features, such as trees, terrain, etc. Natural features are particularly important in recreational vehicle parks where attractive surroundings are one of the most important elements.

Construction Costs. The feasibility study will set an upper limit on construction costs. It is important that final design stay within these construction costs; otherwise, the study will be invalidated.

Maintenance Costs. Final design should give consideration to maintenance costs. Provide accessibility to facilities requiring maintenance so that they can be serviced. Roads should be designed to require a minimum of maintenance and to provide traffic control. Construction should be of quality. In the long run, savings in maintenance will cover the additional cost many times over.

Streets. Street widths must be consistent with the size of the vehicles which will be moving in the park. Thus, a recreational vehicle park would require narrower roads than those in a modern mobile home park: large mobile home units require considerable space for backing. Street construction standards should be consistent with the need to keep maintenance costs low.

Parking. Both guest and recreation area parking must be provided as well as parking at the site. Off-street parking is, of course, to be preferred in both recreational and mobile home parks.

Fire Protection. Careful attention must be given to local codes regulating fire protection facilities.

Sewer Systems. A public sewer into which the park sewer system can empty is, of course, the most desirable situation. However, many mobile home parks and most recreational vehicle parks must provide either septic tank systems or sewage treatment plants because they are usually not in communities where public sewers are available.

Utlities. Design must cover power system, water, gas, telephone, oil, and TV system.

Storm Drains. Flood control, as required by local government, must be carefully studied and provided for in final engineering.

Required Buildings. Complete plans for buildings on the park site as well as plans for each mobile home site must be provided.

Here is a list of the plans that the park architect must supply:

1. A plat plan. This is an accurate boundary survey of the parcel of land to be developed.

2. A topographical map. This is a map showing terrain in one foot gradations on flat land and five foot intervals on steep slopes. The map should show the elevation of existing streets and sidewalks adjacent to the property and should show existing structures on the property. It should show existing storm drains,, utilities, and sanitary systems on or near the property, as well as any easements which may apply.

3. A plot plan similar to that provided in the preliminary survey should be prepared based upon final plot plan design of the park. Additional plot plans should be prepared which show sewer lines, water

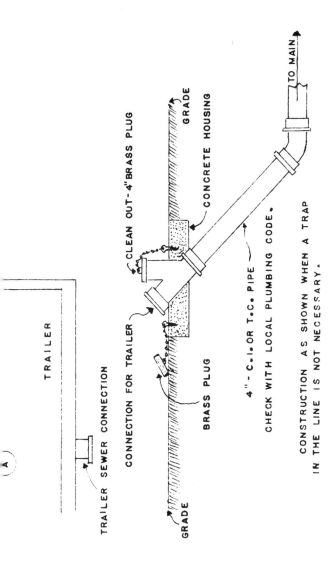

TRAILER

TRAILER SEWER CONNECTION

CONNECTION FOR TRAILER

GRADE

BRASS PLUG

CLEAN OUT - 4" BRASS PLUG

GRADE

CONCRETE HOUSING

TO MAIN

4" - C.I. OR T.C. PIPE

CHECK WITH LOCAL PLUMBING CODE.

CONSTRUCTION AS SHOWN WHEN A TRAP
IN THE LINE IS NOT NECESSARY.

DETAIL SEWER CONNECTION.
NO SCALE

Courtesy: Fred Sparer Co.

Detail drawing of sewer riser at the parking site.

149

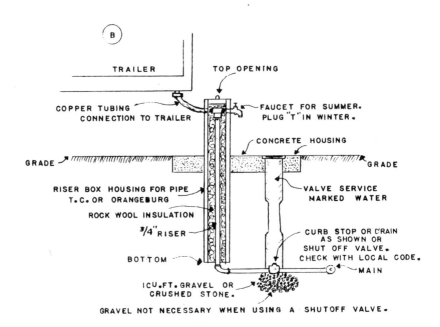

B

TRAILER

TOP OPENING

COPPER TUBING
CONNECTION TO TRAILER

FAUCET FOR SUMMER.
PLUG "T" IN WINTER.

CONCRETE HOUSING

GRADE

GRADE

RISER BOX HOUSING FOR PIPE
T.C. OR ORANGEBURG

VALVE SERVICE
MARKED WATER

ROCK WOOL INSULATION

3/4" RISER

CURB STOP OR DRAIN
AS SHOWN OR
SHUT OFF VALVE.
CHECK WITH LOCAL CODE.

BOTTOM

MAIN

ICU.FT. GRAVEL OR
CRUSHED STONE.

GRAVEL NOT NECESSARY WHEN USING A SHUTOFF VALVE.

DETAIL WATER SERVICE CONNECTION.
NO SCALE

Courtesy: Fred Sparer Co.

Details of a typical water service connection.

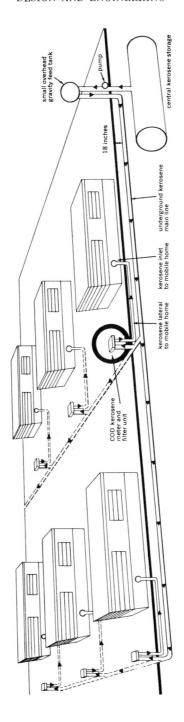

small overhead
gravity feed tank

pump

central kerosene storage

18 inches

underground kerosene
main line

kerosene inlet
to mobile home

kerosene lateral
to mobile home

COD kerosene
meter and
filter unit

Courtesy: Fred Sparer Co.

A central oil distribution system is sometimes included in park plans.

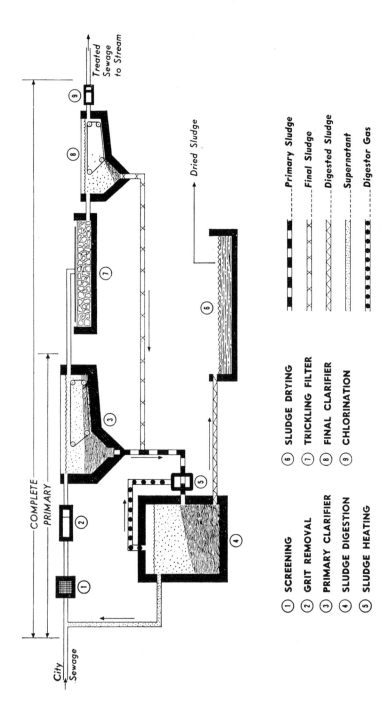

SIMPLIFIED SCHEMATIC SKETCH OF
TYPICAL SEWAGE TREATMENT PLANT

1. SCREENING
2. GRIT REMOVAL
3. PRIMARY CLARIFIER
4. SLUDGE DIGESTION
5. SLUDGE HEATING
6. SLUDGE DRYING
7. TRICKLING FILTER
8. FINAL CLARIFIER
9. CHLORINATION

Primary Sludge
Final Sludge
Digested Sludge
Supernatant
Digestor Gas

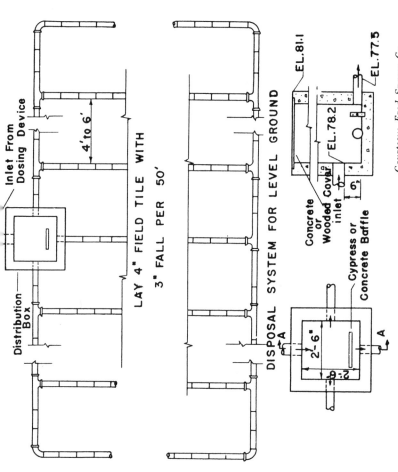

Inlet From Dosing Device

Distribution Box

4' to 6'

LAY 4" FIELD TILE WITH 3" FALL PER 50'

DISPOSAL SYSTEM FOR LEVEL GROUND

EL.81.1

EL.78.2

EL.77.5

Concrete or Wooded Cover

inlet

6"

Cypress or Concrete Baffle

2'-6"

2'-6"

A

A

Courtesy: Fred Sparer Co.

If city sewers are not available plans must provide for sewage treatment plant or a sewage disposal system.

153

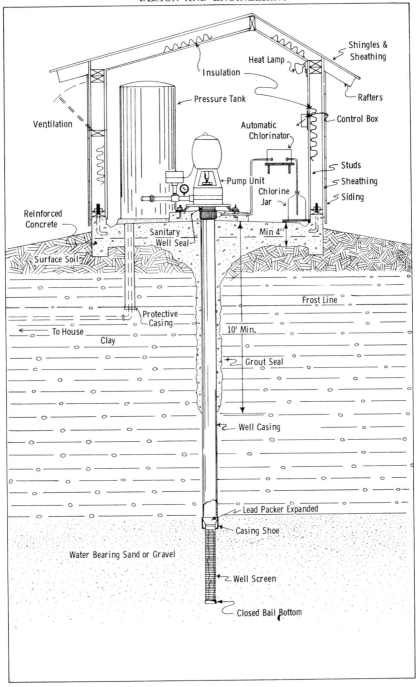

Shingles & Sheathing
Heat Lamp
Insulation
Rafters
Pressure Tank
Control Box
Ventilation
Automatic Chlorinator
Studs
Sheathing
Siding
Pump Unit
Chlorine Jar
Reinforced Concrete
Sanitary Well Seal
Min 4"
Surface Soil
Frost Line
Protective Casing
To House
10' Min.
Clay
Grout Seal
Well Casing
Lead Packer Expanded
Casing Shoe
Water Bearing Sand or Gravel
Well Screen
Closed Bail Bottom

If wells are the source for water plans for the well, pump house, and water storage must be provided.

lines, gas lines, TV lines, and telephone lines super-imposed upon the plot plan. This may require several additional plot plans to eliminate confusion concerning the various utility lines.

4. If water is to be obtained from wells, the plans should show the details of the well system, the well house, and any water storage facility.

5. A complete grading and drainage plan should be provided.

6. Buildings. Detailed plans should be provided for the recreation room, service facilities, offices, and any other buildings.

7. If the park is to use fuel oil distribution system for mobile home heaters, an oil distribution system should be superimposed on the plot plan.

8. If a swimming pool is to be provided, pool plans should be provided.

9. Recreation facilities such as children's playgrounds, shuffleboard courts, volleyball courts, tennis court, horseshoe courts, etc. should be detailed by plans.

10. Mobile home or recreational vehicle individual lot plans should be provided, showing the improvements which will be provided on each individual lot.

11. If landscaping is a considerable item, there should be detailed drawings for use by landscape contractors.

12. Additional plans may also be required, depending upon local regulations. Thus you will frequently be required to show plans for roads, walks, curbs, street lighting, etc.

During the drawing of the final plans very careful attention must be paid to local park codes. Many communities have regulations which may be obtained from the building department. These must, of course, be strictly adhered to. It is the responsibility of the architect and engineer to see that the final plans conform with local regulations.

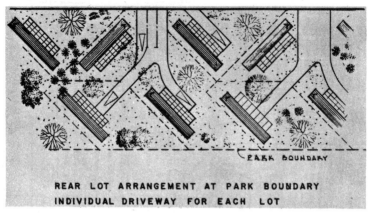

REAR LOT ARRANGEMENT AT PARK BOUNDARY
INDIVIDUAL DRIVEWAY FOR EACH LOT

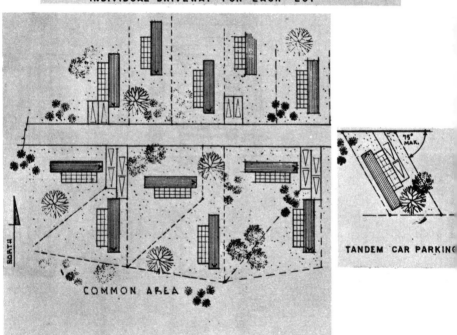

VARIOUS COMBINATIONS. AN ORDERLY SCHEME WITHOUT
MONOTONY. GENERAL ORIENTATION TOWARD SOUTHWEST

TANDEM CAR PARKING

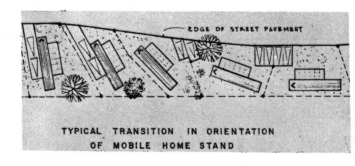

TYPICAL TRANSITION IN ORIENTATION
OF MOBILE HOME STAND

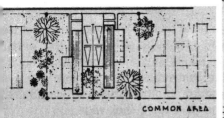

RONT YARD & REAR YARD ORIENTAION,
OMBINED UTILITY CORE & CAR
ARKING, BIG SIDE YARD

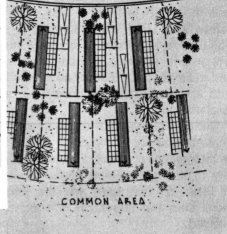

FRONT YARD & REAR YARD ORIENTATION.
DEEP LOTS.
HIGH DENSITY POSSIBLE

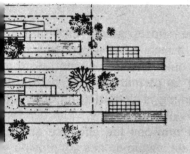

REAR LOT ARRANGEMENT. OVERALL HIGH
DENSITY COMBINED WITH SPACIOUS GROUPING

TANDEM & PARALLEL
CAR PARKING

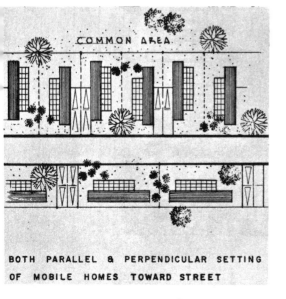

BOTH PARALLEL & PERPENDICULAR SETTING
OF MOBILE HOMES TOWARD STREET

KEY

◼ ← FRONT
MOBILE HOME STAND

PATIO

CAR PARKING

LOT LINE & MARKER

Typical mobile home modules and arrangements.

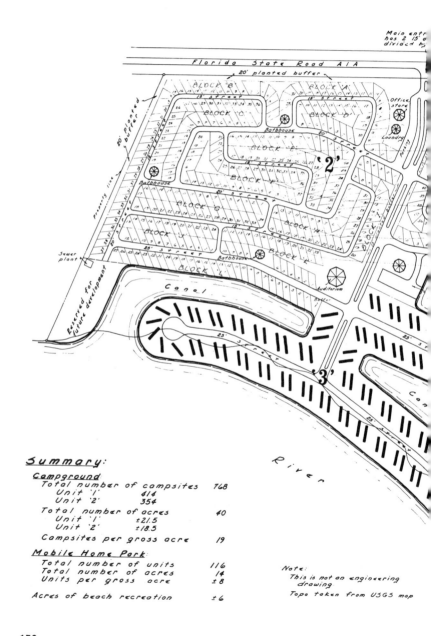

Proposed Site Plan
Campground, Mobile H

Florida State Road A1A
20' planted buffer

BLOCK B   BLOCK A

BLOCK C   BLOCK D   Office store

Bathhouse   Laundry

BLOCK E   '2'

Bathhouse   BLOCK F

BLOCK G   BLOCK H

BLOCK J   BLOCK K

Sewer plant

Bathhouse   Auditorium

BLOCK

Canal

'3'

River

Summary:

Campground
Total number of campsites	768
Unit '1'	414
Unit '2'	354
Total number of acres	40
Unit '1'	±21.5
Unit '2'	±18.5
Campsites per gross acre	19

Mobile Home Park:
Total number of units	116
Total number of acres	14
Units per gross acre	±8
Acres of beach recreation	±6

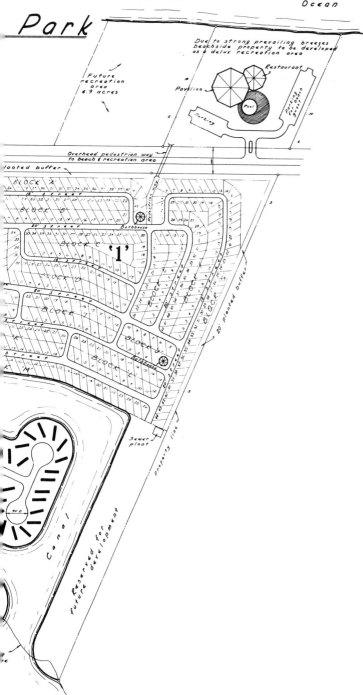

Courtesy: *Mobile Homes Manufacturers Association*
Plot plan for a combination mobile home and recreational vehicle park.

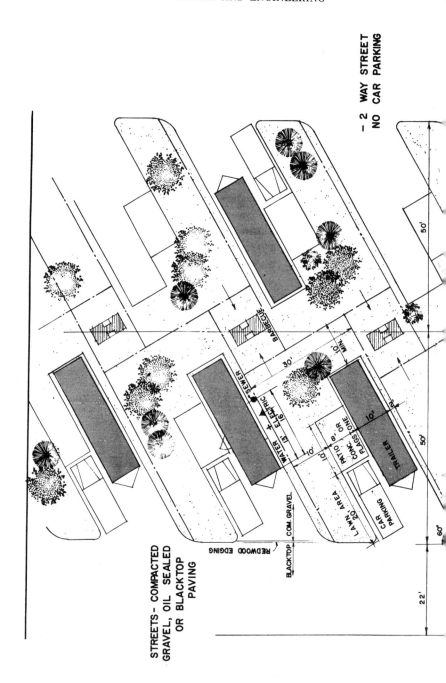

STREETS - COMPACTED
GRAVEL, OIL SEALED
OR BLACKTOP
PAVING

REDWOOD EDGING

BLACKTOP COM. GRAVEL

SEWER

WATER 13 16 ELECTRIC

BARBECUE

30'

10' MIN.

PATIO 8' OR
CONC. OR
FLAGSTONE

10'

10'

LAWN AREA
20'

CAR
PARKING

TRAILER

10'

10'

50'

50'

60'

22'

- 2 WAY STREET
NO CAR PARKING

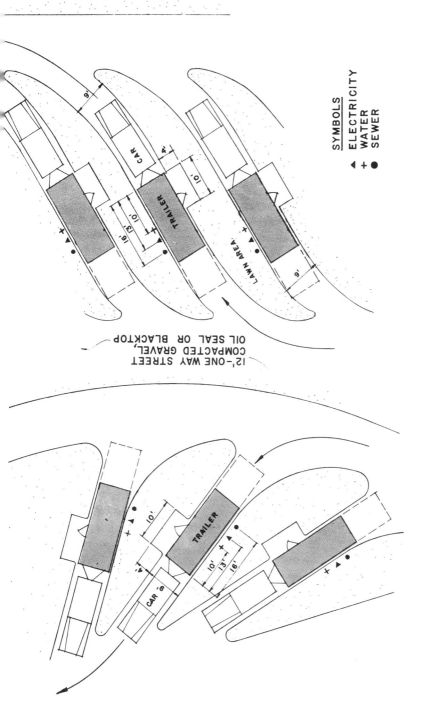

SYMBOLS
▲ ELECTRICITY
+ WATER
● SEWER

Typical recreational vehicle space design provides for either "drive-thru" or "back in" parking.

161

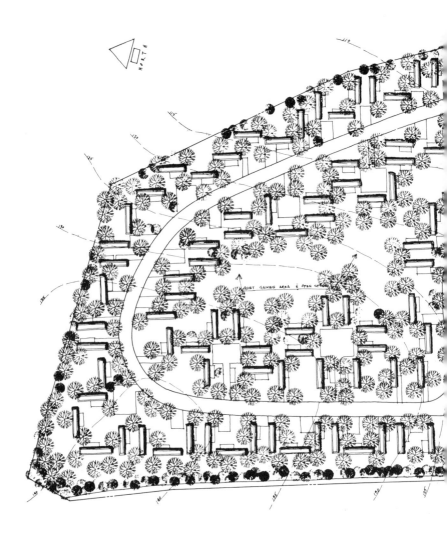

LAKE AMAH-LEE

OPEN SPACE & GAMES

PARKING APPROX. 40-50 CARS

FUTURE AREA
FOR SWIMMING POOL,
CABANAS, ETC.

NOTE: LOCATE SEWAGE
DISPOSAL PLANT SOUTHWEST
OF THIS AREA WELL
SCREENED FROM ROAD.

GROSS AREA MOBILE HOME PARK :   APPROX. 25 AC.
NO. MOBILE HOME LOTS :   172
DENSITY :   6.5 TO 7.0 ±

A 172 space mobile home park plot plan.

Topography drawing.

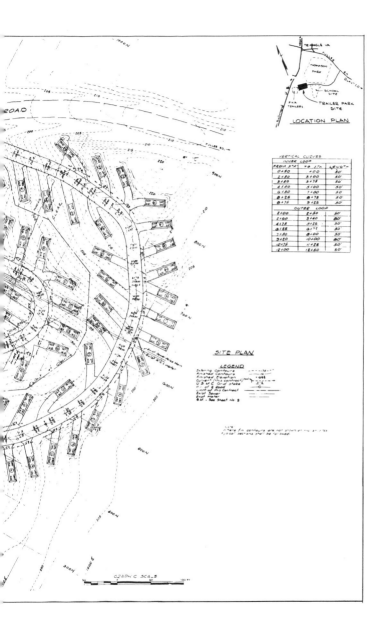

SITE PLAN

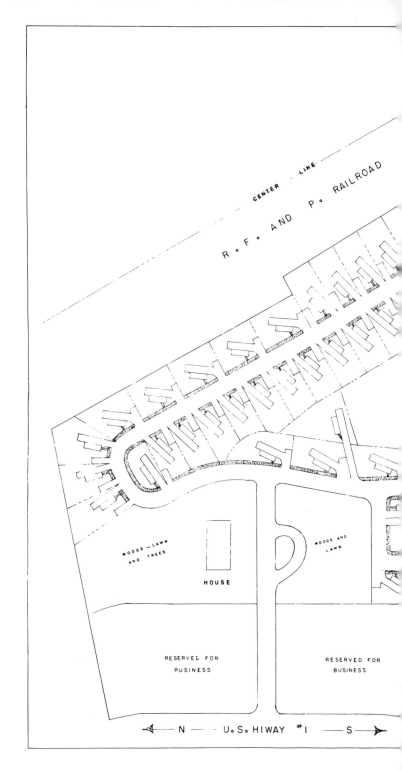

MOBILE HOME COURT
12.92 ACRES – 90 SPACES

BY.– FRED SPARER CO.
Specialists-MOBILE HOME COURTS.

LOT TABULATION

Type		Number	%
A		232	73%
B		60	19%
C		27	8%
	TOTAL	319	100%

LOT TABULATION (FUTURE)

Type	Number	%
A	46	74%
B	8	13%
C	8	13%
	62	100%

TOTAL ACREAGE:	39 ±
TOTAL ACREAGE FUTURE:	8 ±
SITES PER ACRE:	7.8
SITES PER ACRE FUTURE:	7.8
MAIN RECREATION AREA:	1.8 Acres
STORAGE & OTHER RECREATION:	1.3 Acres
GUEST PARKING:	70

Courtesy: Marquis & Associates

A plot plan for a 319 space mobile home park.

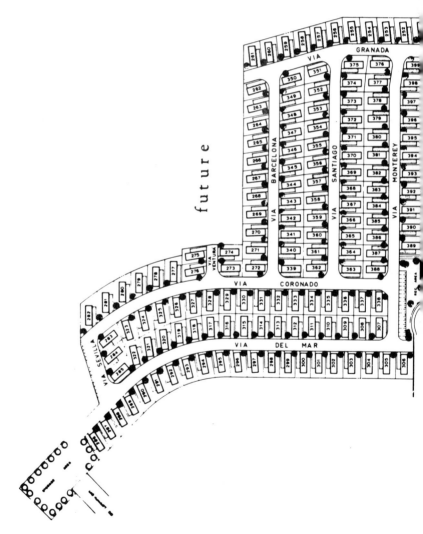

future

• 400 UNITS

A plot plan for a 400 space mobile home park.

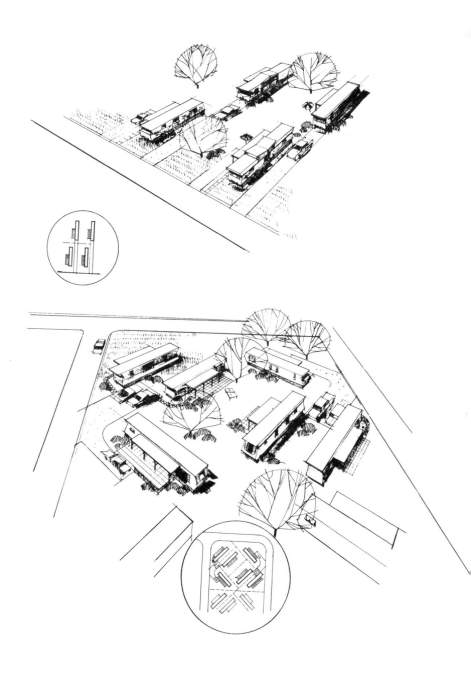

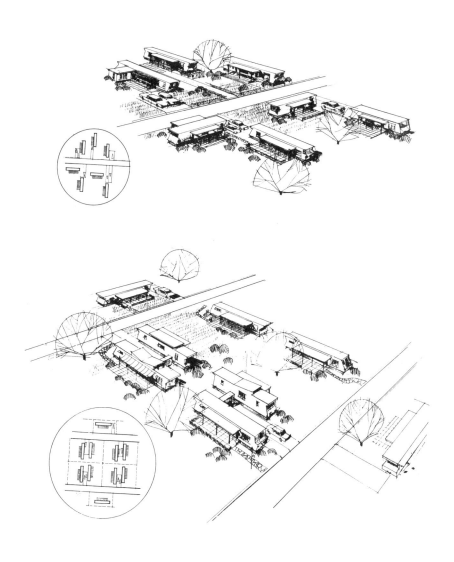

Courtesy: Mobile Homes Manufacturers Association
Pictorial illustrations of mobile home park modules.

NOTICE

THIS WATER FOR FLUSHING AND CLEANING PURPOSE ONLY

#(APPROVED SOURCE AS INDICATED BY LOCATION)

VACUUM BREAKER

WATER TOWER

ATTACH SIGN TO POST OR FENCE

SIGN B

SHUT-OFF VALVE

WATER NOZZLE (WITHOUT VALVE)

1¼" TEE & PLUG

1¼" PIPE SLEEVE

SERVICE BOX

FROST LINE

3-WAY COCK W/ EXTENSION HANDLE

4" C.I. OR VITRIFIED SOIL PIPE

HATCH CONNECT W/ 4" C.I. NIPPLE

1'-6" MIN.

8"

TRAILERS
HOLDING TANK DISPOSAL INSTRUCTIONS

CONNECT YOUR HOSE TO HOLDING TANK – PLACE END SECURELY IN DRAIN OPENING WHILE HOLDING COVER OPEN WITH FOOT.
OPEN TRAILER TANK DRAIN VALVE.
FLUSH AWAY ANY SPILLAGE ON CONCRETE INTO DRAIN.

SIGN A

2'-0"

1'-8"

VIEW B

GRAVITY DRAIN

LOT LINE

½" DRAIN UP

CONTROL VALVE ACCESS COVER

WATER TOWER SEE DETAIL 1

VIEW A

1'-8"

1'-8"

SIGN

4" x 4" WOOD BUMPER

5" THICK CONCRETE TROWEL SMOOTH

ASPHALT OR GRAVEL

VIEW A

2'-0"

2'-0"

HATCH SEE DET. 2

4'-0"

SLOPE 3/4" TO DRAIN

5'-0" MIN.

2'-6"

7'-6"

5'-0"

VIEW A

VIEW B

PLAN

174

Details of a sanitary station.

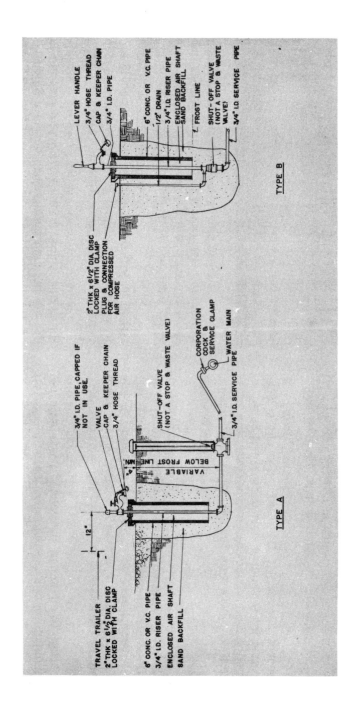

Details of water riser pipe for a recreational vehicle park.

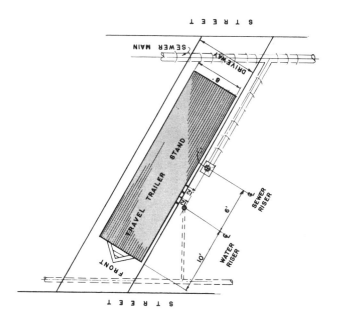

Recommended location of water and sewer riser pipes for a recreational vehicle parking stand.

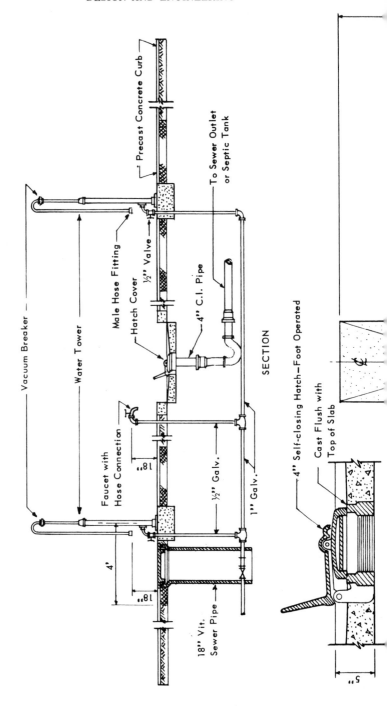

Vacuum Breaker

Water Tower

Precast Concrete Curb

Male Hose Fitting

Hatch Cover

½" Valve

To Sewer Outlet
or Septic Tank

4" C.I. Pipe

Faucet with
Hose Connection

18"

½" Galv.

1" Galv.

4'

18"

18" Vit.
Sewer Pipe

SECTION

4" Self-closing Hatch—Foot Operated

Cast Flush with
Top of Slab

5"

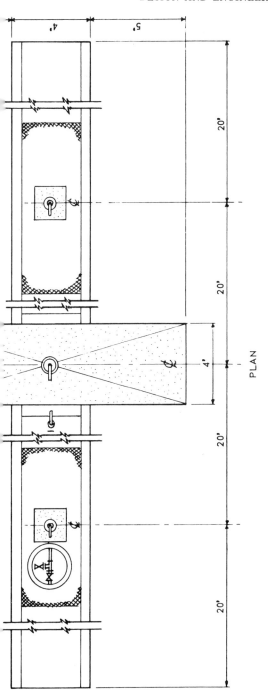

PLAN

Recreational vehicle parks require a sanitary dumping station to service self-contained recreational vehicles.

0'   4'   8'

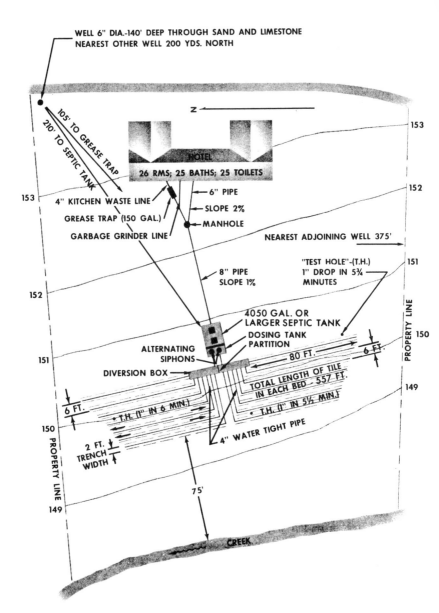

Figure 24.—Typical layout plan of a subsurface sewage-disposal system.

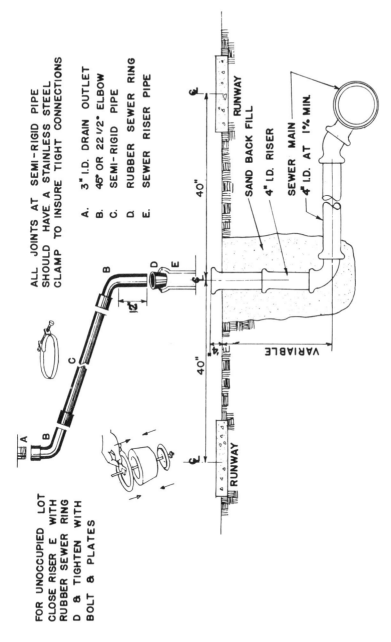

ALL JOINTS AT SEMI-RIGID PIPE
SHOULD HAVE A STAINLESS STEEL
CLAMP TO INSURE TIGHT CONNECTIONS

A. 3" I.D. DRAIN OUTLET
B. 45° OR 22 1/2° ELBOW
C. SEMI-RIGID PIPE
D. RUBBER SEWER RING
E. SEWER RISER PIPE

FOR UNOCCUPIED LOT
CLOSE RISER E WITH
RUBBER SEWER RING
D & TIGHTEN WITH
BOLT & PLATES

RUNWAY

SAND BACK FILL

4" I.D. RISER

SEWER MAIN

4" I.D. AT 1% MIN.

40"

40"

VARIABLE

RUNWAY

12"

Typical sewer service connection.

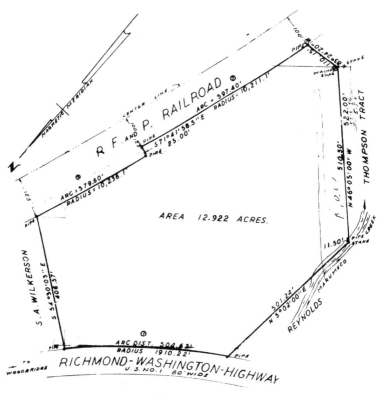

PLAT
SHOWING SURVEY
OF A PARCEL OF LAND

CURVE TABLE						
	DELTA	RADIUS	TAN	ARC	CH	CH BEARING
①	15°08'08"	1910.22	253.78	504.62	503.16	N 40°29'16"E
②②	2°07'24"	10,236.10	189.82	379.60	379.58	S 70°21'44"W
③	3°21'08"	10,211.10	298.80	597.44	597.14	S6°57'77'54"W

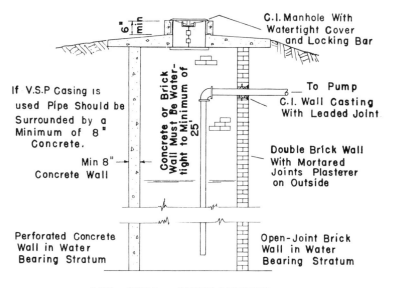

If V.S.P Casing is used Pipe Should be Surrounded by a Minimum of 8" Concrete.

Min 8" Concrete Wall

Perforated Concrete Wall in Water Bearing Stratum

C.I. Manhole With Watertight Cover and Locking Bar

To Pump
C.I. Wall Casting With Leaded Joint

Double Brick Wall With Mortared Joints Plasterer on Outside

Open-Joint Brick Wall in Water Bearing Stratum

DUG WELL DEVELOPMENT

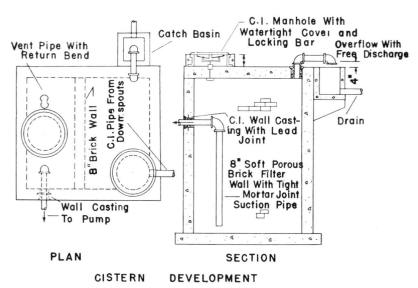

Vent Pipe With Return Bend

Catch Basin

C.I. Manhole With Watertight Cover and Locking Bar

Overflow With Free Discharge

Drain

C.I. Wall Casting With Lead Joint

8" Soft Porous Brick Filter Wall With Tight Mortar Joint Suction Pipe

Wall Casting To Pump

PLAN

SECTION

CISTERN DEVELOPMENT

DUG WELL AND CISTERN DEVELOPMENT

Courtesy: Fred Sparer Co.
Plans must include details for well development if city water is not available.

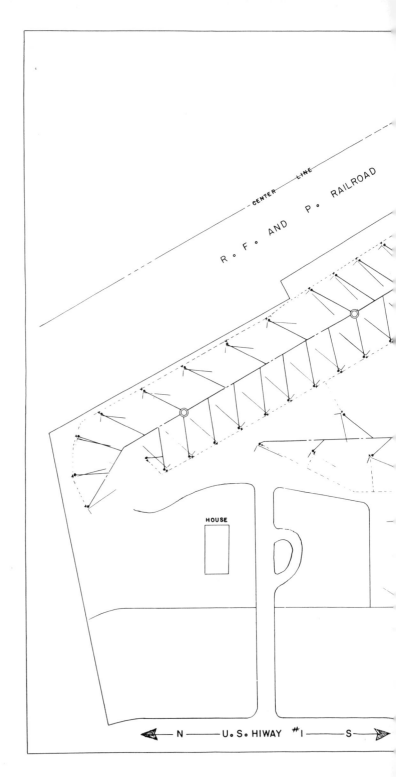

CENTER LINE

R. F. AND P. RAILROAD

HOUSE

N —— U. S. HIWAY #1 —— S

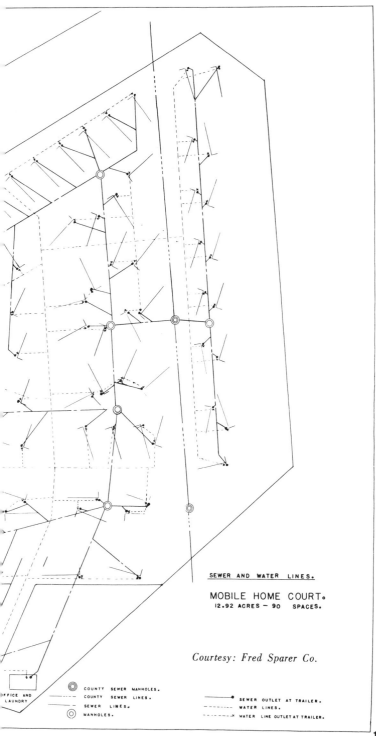

SEWER AND WATER LINES.

MOBILE HOME COURT.
12.92 ACRES — 90 SPACES.

Courtesy: Fred Sparer Co.

OFFICE AND
LAUNDRY

◎	COUNTY SEWER MANHOLES.	
	COUNTY SEWER LINES.	
	SEWER LINES.	
◎	MANHOLES.	

SEWER OUTLET AT TRAILER.
WATER LINES.
WATER LINE OUTLET AT TRAILER.

185

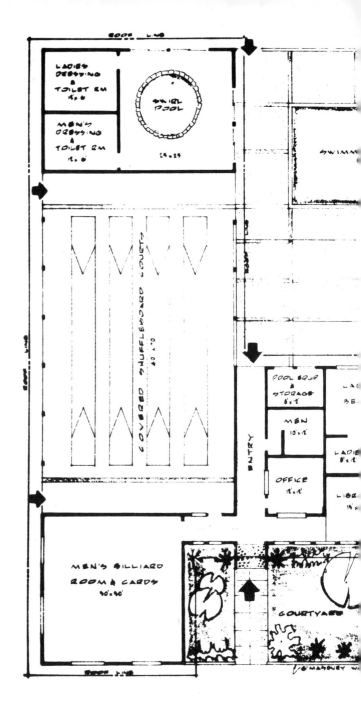

LADIES
DRESSING
&
TOILET RM
16'.0"

MEN'S
DRESSING
&
TOILET RM
19'.0"

SWIRL
POOL

29'.29'

SWIMM

COVERED SHUFFLEBOARD COURTS
40'.0'

EDGE LINE

EDGE LINE

ENTRY

ENTRY

POOL EQUIP
&
STORAGE
8'.12'

MEN
10'.12'

OFFICE
13'.12'

LA
3E

LADIE
8'.12'

LIBR
14'.

MEN'S BILLIARD
ROOM & CARDS
30'.30'

COURTYARD

6" MASONRY W

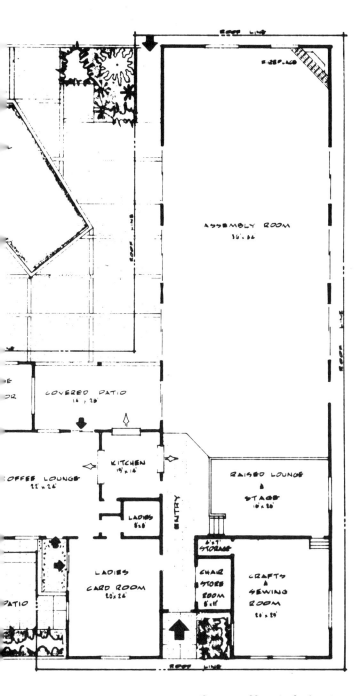

ASSEMBLY ROOM
36' x 66'

FIREPLACE

COVERED PATIO
14' x 28'

KITCHEN
10' x 16'

RAISED LOUNGE
&
STAGE
18' x 28'

OFFEE LOUNGE
22' x 26'

LADIES
8' x 8'

ENTRY

6' x 7'
STORAGE

LADIES
CARD ROOM
20' x 26'

CHAIR
STORE
ROOM
8' x 14'

CRAFTS
&
SEWING
ROOM
20' x 29'

PATIO

ROOF LINE

Courtesy: Marquis & Associates

Floor plan a 12,000 square foot club house.

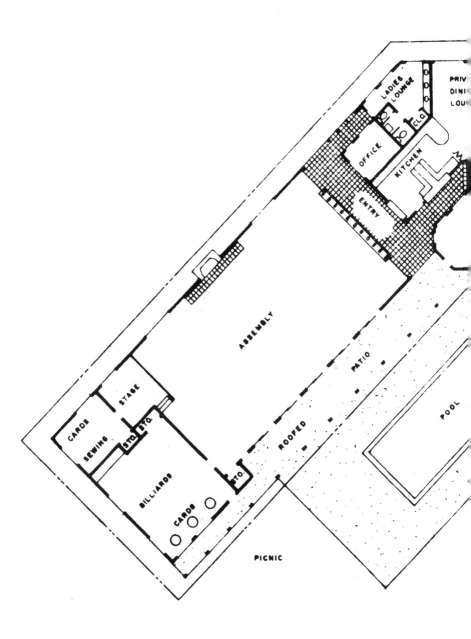

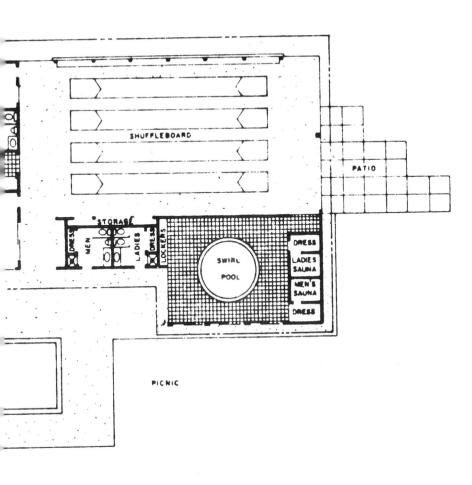

Courtesy: Marquis & Associates
Floor plan for a 17,000 square foot club house.

189

This visitor center–museum building provides office space for ranger interpretive staff. Main entrance is via the terrace entrance on the northeast corner; a loggia extending from the southeast corner leads to a utility building behind the visitor center. A mechanical room, separating the museum from the toilet rooms, opens to the west side of the building and provides space for heating and air conditioning equipment, hot water heater, and entrance to a plumber's alley for the repair and maintenance of sewer and water lines.

FLOOR PLAN

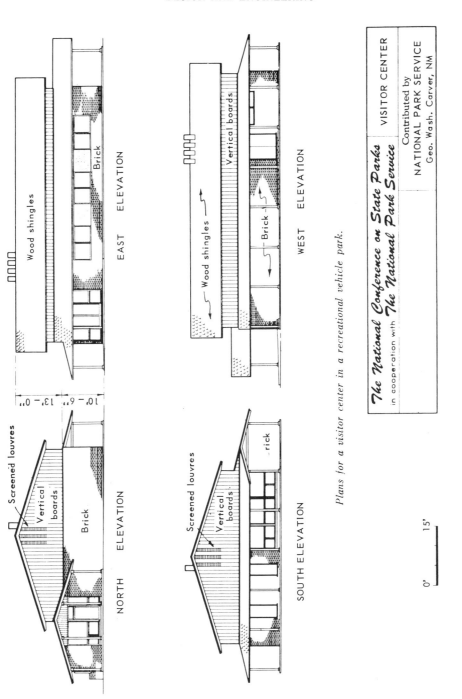

Plans for a visitor center in a recreational vehicle park.

EAST ELEVATION

Wood shingles

Brick

WEST ELEVATION

Vertical boards

Wood shingles

Brick

NORTH ELEVATION

Screened louvres

Vertical boards

Brick

SOUTH ELEVATION

Screened louvres

Vertical boards

rick

13'-0" 10'-6"

VISITOR CENTER

The National Conference on State Parks
in cooperation with *The National Park Service*

Contributed by
NATIONAL PARK SERVICE
Geo. Wash. Carver, NM

0'   15'

Details of a service building for a recreational vehicle park.

Typical mobile home stand.

193

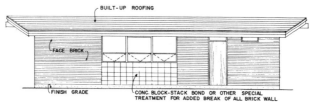

BUILT-UP ROOFING

FACE BRICK

FINISH GRADE

CONC. BLOCK-STACK BOND OR OTHER SPECIAL TREATMENT FOR ADDED BREAK OF ALL BRICK WALL

SIDE ELEVATION
NO SCALE

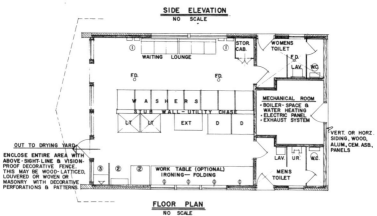

WAITING LOUNGE

STOR. CAB.

WOMENS TOILET
F.D.
LAV.   WC

F.D.   F.D.

W A S H E R S

STUB WALL-UTILITY CHASE

LT   LT   EXT   D   D

MECHANICAL ROOM
• BOILER-SPACE & WATER HEATING
• ELECTRIC PANEL
• EXHAUST SYSTEM

VERT. OR HORZ. SIDING, WOOD, ALUM., CEM. ASB., PANELS

OUT TO DRYING YARD

ENCLOSE ENTIRE AREA WITH ABOVE-SIGHT-LINE & VISION-PROOF DECORATIVE FENCE. THIS MAY BE WOOD-LATTICED, LOUVERED OR WOVEN OR MASONRY WITH DECORATIVE PERFORATIONS & PATTERNS.

③   ②   ②   WORK TABLE (OPTIONAL) IRONING— FOLDING

LAV.   UR.   W.C.

MENS TOILET

FLOOR PLAN
NO SCALE

SYMBOLS

W – WASHER
LT- LAUNDRY TRAY, DOUBLE
D - DRYER
EXT-COMMERCIAL EXTRACTOR
SS- SERVICE SINK
⊕ WALL OUTLETS
① DISPENSER-DETERGENT, SOAP, STARCH, BLUING, BLEACH, ETC
② DISPENSER, CANDY, DRINKS, ETC. (OPTIONAL)
③ TELEPHONE

ABBREVIATIONS

W.C.   WATER CLOSET
UR.   URINAL
LAV.   LAVATORY
F.D.   FLOOR DRAIN

INTERIOR ROOM FINISHES

	MINIMUM	GOOD
FLOOR	CONCRETE ✱	CERAMIC TILE OR TERRAZZO
BASE	COVED CONC. ✱	COVED CERAMIC TILE, FACING TILE OR TERRAZZO
WALLS	CEMENT ENAMEL OR EPOXY SPRAYED ON CONC. BLOCK.	CERAMIC TILE OR FACING TILE
CEILING	CEM. PLASTER	MINERAL ACOUSTICAL TILE .

✱ WITH HARDENER ADDITIVE

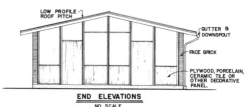

LOW PROFILE ROOF PITCH

GUTTER & DOWNSPOUT

FACE BRICK

PLYWOOD, PORCELAIN, CERAMIC TILE OR OTHER DECORATIVE PANEL.

END ELEVATIONS
NO SCALE

194

TYPICAL MINIMUM LAUNDRY BUILDING FACILITIES
FOR A MOBILE HOME PARK OF ABOUT 100 SPACES

CHECK OWN PARK DEMANDS BY LOCAL INVESTIGATIONS OF:

1. AVAILABLE COMMUNITY FACILITIES NEARBY.
2. NUMBER OF COACHES WITH OWN LAUNDRY FACILITIES.
   (THE NUMBER OF UNITS MANUFACTURED WITH LAUNDRY
   FACILITIES IS GROWING EACH YEAR.)
3. SEASONAL AND WEATHER CONDITIONS TO ESTABLISH RATIO
   OF WASHERS TO DRYERS- AND TENANT PREFERENCES FOR EITHER
   OR BOTH TYPES OF DRYING.
4. DEMAND FOR ADDITIONAL LAUNDRY SERVICES OR SPACE SUCH AS
   IRONING, HANDLING, PACKAGING ETC.
5. COMPARE COSTS AND/OR NEED FOR COMMERCIAL-TYPE EXTRACTORS
   & DRYERS.

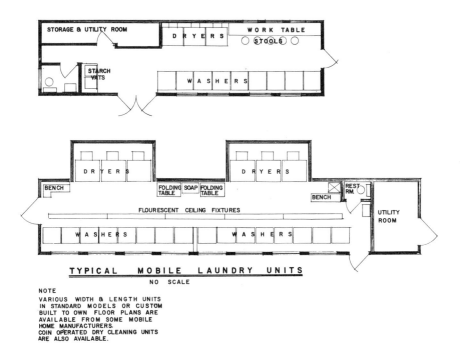

TYPICAL MOBILE LAUNDRY UNITS
NO SCALE

NOTE
VARIOUS WIDTH & LENGTH UNITS
IN STANDARD MODELS OR CUSTOM
BUILT TO OWN FLOOR PLANS ARE
AVAILABLE FROM SOME MOBILE
HOME MANUFACTURERS.
COIN OPERATED DRY CLEANING UNITS
ARE ALSO AVAILABLE.

Courtesy: Mobile Homes Manufacturers Association
Typical laundry building.

CONSTRUCTION

The first step in getting the park actually constructed is a complete set of working drawings and specifications which will have been prepared by your architect. These drawings and specifications are submitted to contractors who are interested in bidding on the project.

Local industry associations are usually helpful in steering you to contractors with experience in park construction. Your architect can probably suggest contractors who should be asked to bid. You can ask the architect to do a "takeoff" on the plans and specifications, giving you his estimate of park construction cost. You can compare bids you receive with the architect's takeoff if you wish.

The Contractor

The contractor to whom you award the job may or may not be the lowest bidder. The selection of a contractor involves considerations other than cost. A contractor with whom you consider doing business should be requested to supply references. You should ask to look at other projects he has completed. Have your banker check his credit standing and reputation in the community. The contractor should be required to supply a completion bond, and your contract should provide a date by which the project must be completed, with penalties if the contractor fails to meet that deadline. The usual penalty provided in such contracts is that the contractor must pay any additional interest you must pay on the construction loan as a result of his failure to complete the project by the deadline.

Insurance

Insurance coverage during the period of construction is extremely important. Your contractor should be required to carry liability insurance which protects him as well as you. You should require certification in writing from the contractor's insurance company that he is so covered before he begins work. For a nominal sum your insurance broker can cover you in case there is negligence on the part of the contractor, or any of the sub-contractors, to carry the insurance required. This is one place where you should not try to save. Be sure insurance is placed with a strong company and that you are fully protected. One small accident for which you are not covered could wipe out your investment.

Lien Laws

Carefully protect yourself against lien laws. Such laws provide that any worker, contractor, or subcontractor who may have done work on a piece of property for which he has not been paid has a right to file a lien against that property. This law not infrequently leads to a situation where an owner may have paid the general contractor, but the general contractor has failed to pay all of his bills, resulting in liens being filed against the property. If the general contractor is unable to pay, you may be forced to pay a second time in order to clear up the lien against your property. All liens, of course, cloud the title to property, and it cannot be transferred unless such lien is cleared up. To protect yourself it is customary to require the contractor to deliver to you a waiver of lien executed by all who have been connected with the project. Your attorney will assist you in this.

Progress Payments

An excellent service for an owner in improving property is that offered by many commercial banks who finance the construction. Inquire at the commercial bank financing your construction about their ability to handle all of the details of making progress payments to the contractor. They will provide inspection of the site to be sure that work is progressing satisfactorily, will collect the required liens from the contractor, and will make payments to him only insofar as these matters are satisfactory.

Construction Supervision

Architects charge a fee for designing and engineering a project, and many will also accept an additional fee for supervising the project. Often an owner, in an effort to save this additional fee, will attempt to supervise the project himself. Unless you are experienced in the contracting or building field it is wise to pay the architect the additional fee required so that he will supervise the project.

Changing Plans

Even though your architect has been very careful in preparing the plans and engineering, as the work progresses, you may want to make some changes. In some cases the contractor himself may make a suggestion as to changes. Caution must be exercised at this point for you will increase the cost of the contract by making changes not originally specified in the bid submitted by the contractor. Just be sure that you have in writing the exact cost of any changes you order. When you are planning a park, it is wise to set aside a sum for contingencies.

Local Laws

One protection you have in developing a project is that it must conform with the building codes of the community in which it is constructed. The site will therefore be frequently visited by inspectors who will make sure construction is in accordance with local codes. Payments should not be made to contractors until construction has been certified.

FINANCING

A park requires two types of financing. First, financing is required during the construction period. Second, there is long term mortgage financing. Construction financing will not be available until such time as you have arranged for long term financing. The financial institution which will provide long term mortgage financing provides you with a "letter of intent." This indicates to the firm providing construction financing that when the park is completed, someone stands ready to pay them and assume the obligations accumulated during the construction phase.

Construction Financing

Construction financing is usually for a period of one year and, in exceptional cases, two years. The usual source for funds for construction financing is commercial banks. Other sources are available, and those with whom you negotiate for long term financing are often able to direct and guide you to firms who can supply construction financing.

Long Term Financing

The investment you make in a proposed project should be held to a minimum until such time as you have assurance that you can obtain long term financing. Long term financing is frequently the most difficult hurdle; in some cases it may prove to be an obstacle which cannot be overcome. Your option to purchase a specific parcel of land for park development should therefore be conditional upon your ability to obtain financing. The tool which is used to shop for financing is a professionally prepared feasibility study. This is an expense to which you must normally commit yourself before you can obtain financing. The feasibility study contains the marketing data on the proposed project and the financial projections that financial institutions require before committing themselves to loans. A poorly prepared study can result in inability to obtain a loan.

The amount which you can borrow, the interest rate, and additional fees which you may pay for obtaining the loan, are dependent upon the money market at the time you are shopping. If money is tight, considerable shopping may be necessary to find a financial institution with funds available, and with sufficient interest in the project to accommodate you. On the other hand, if loan money is plentiful, then it is desirable to shop carefully to obtain the best possible terms.

The amount which you can borrow is somewhere between 75 and 90 percent of the total value of the completed park, computed by adding the value of the land to the cost of the construction work. For example:

Cost of Land
20 Acres @ $5,000 per acre $100,000
Cost of Development
160 Spaces @ $2,500 per space $400,000
                        Total Cost of Project $500,000

If Loan is 75% You Borrow $375,000
If Loan is 90% You Borrow $450,000

Sources

Saving and loan associations are excellent sources. Many of these associations have had excellent experience with park loans and invested substantial amounts of their available loan funds in this industry. Insurance companies are also large investors in the park industry. This is also true of pension funds.

FHA Financing

The Federal Housing Administration has announced a program for financing parks. They provide financing to the extent of $500,000 on the basis of loaning up to 90 percent of the cost of the project with an upper limit of $2600 per space for development. FHA loans run as long as 40 years. Of course FHA loans are obtained through regular financial institutions with the FHA insuring the loan. To discover the institutions which work with FHA you should contact your regional FHA office. The advantage of FHA loans is that they assure the banker security for his loan. The disadvantages are: (1) the banker is often limited to the amount of interest which he can charge and he may not want to loan funds at that rate of interest; (2) any loan under FHA insurance involves a considerable amount of red tape. To some extent this red tape may be worth the effort since FHA inspection is an added assurance that the park will be properly constructed by your contractor.

Mortgage Brokers

Every community has mortgage brokers. These are usually listed in the yellow section of the phone book under the title Mortgage Loans or Mortgage Brokers. These are individuals who have contact with many sources of capital. If you are unable to obtain a loan through normal channels, such as contacting savings and loans or insurance companies, then it may be advisable to contact a mortgage broker. He can review your project and submit it to various financial institutions with whom he works. He receives from the lender a small fee for his services. Some mortgage brokers will advise you that they will make an effort to obtain a loan for you, provided you will guarantee them a specific fee; it is not recommended that you deal with this type of mortgage brokerage firm. Most reputable firms expect to receive a fee only from the lender, and only after obtaining the required financing.

Other Sources

There are several other sources available to you in seeking possible loan funds. The industry associations in your community will usually have a list of lenders who are interested in loaning money to those who are building parks. The architect with whom you work and the contractor with whom you will be working are often good sources for leads for long term mortgage loans.

Syndication

One final method of financing a park deserves special attention. Parks require a substantial amount of equity capital. The real estate syndicate is a practical method for raising this substantial equity money. This book is not the place to discuss syndication in detail; lengthy books are written on the subject. But, briefly the procedure is as follows.

The developer finds and options the land to be developed. He has a feasability study prepared. A limited partnership is formed with the developer being the general partner. Limited partnerships are sold to investors in units of $5,000 to $25,000 to raise the equity capital required. The park is then built and managed by the developer — the general partner.

The advantages to the limited partner are:
1. Risk is limited to original investment.
2. He participates in a large real estate development with no management responsibility and with a relatively small investment.
3. As a partner he has a tax advantage. Depreciation to him is in proportion to his investment, thus sheltering income.
4. Because his investment is in real estate it is relatively secure.
5. If the project is later sold he is in a capital gains position with its tax advantages.

The advantages to the general partner are:
1. He can raise the equity capital the project requires.
2. He receives fees and/or equity for putting the project together.
3. He receives a management fee.
4. He participates in earnings and/or profits in case of sale.

The prospective investor in a park syndicate should be sure that the developer is thoroughly qualified to successfully develop and operate a park either because of his own park industry experience and knowledge or the retention of professionals in the industry to assure the required experience and knowledge.

PARK MANAGEMENT

Introduction

I have emphasized before that the keys to a successful park are location, plant, and management. Having dealt with location and plant, let's consider management.

Keep in mind that this book is designed to give you an overall view of the park industry; a detailed discussion of management is quite out of place here. The introduction indicates that I am co-authoring a publication on this subject which will probably run several thousand pages, and which is not to be available for another year to two years. But since management is a key element in the success of a park, it would be negligent not to touch upon the subject in this publication.

Those who are uninitiated to the park industry are frequently of the opinion that park management should be a relatively simple undertaking. Nothing could be further from the truth. An excellent plant in an excellent location which is poorly managed almost never succeeds if well managed competitive parks have vacancies. Successful management involves solving almost an unlimited number of problems; proficiency in solving these problems comes either through experience or proper training, or both. I am associated with a school which trains individuals for both mobile home and recreational vehicle park management on a correspondence basis. The school has students all over the United States. If there is one universal statement made by those who graduate from the course, it is that they failed to realize before they took the course how much was involved; that had they failed to take the course, they would have surely failed to succeed in the field of park management. The school involves itself in consulting work for the park industry. A major part of that consulting work involves consultation with owners who have an unsuccessful operation primarily because management of the park is inadequate. Don't under-estimate the importance of management — it is vital to success. Don't under-estimate the complexity — oversimplification will most surely lead to many problems which will reflect themselves in a less than best return on the owner's park investment.

The average park being developed in the United States at the present times represents an investment in the vicinity of one-half to one million dollars. Such investment should be protected by having it administered by management that is trained and/or experienced. Only in this way can the investor be sure that his investment is fully protected and that it earns a rate of return commensurate with opportunities available to investors in the park industry. Let us proceed now to list the categories of knowledge in which a park manager must be proficient and make some comments with reference to each category.

Park Promotion

Promotion for a new park should begin before it is completed. A manager should be retained two to three months before the park is ready to accept its first tenants.

The basic tool used for promotion is as in other industries, the satisfied customer. If the first residents are satisfied and happy in the park, they will be most anxious to encourage their friends to join them in their congenial atmosphere. There are a multitude of techniques available to the manager to assure resident satisfaction. We shall list only some of them here. They are:

1. Knowledge of the park industry and the vehicles which are placed in the park. A manager is frequently called upon for advice and counsel from residents who expect him to be an expert. He needs industry knowledge in order to properly service those inquiries.

2. The manager must know how to successfully deal with all elements in the community in which the park is located. Community acceptance and endorse-

ment of the park is important so that the residents of the park will be received favorably, and also so that the community will recommend the park to those who may be prospective residents.

3. The manager must know how to establish himself as the manager when he is first hired. He must understand to what extent he can properly exert his authority without developing a poor public image for himself.

4. There is a long list of techniques which management uses to build a fine relationship with residents. The manager must know of these techniques and how to apply them.

5. A successful manager must know specifically how he can work with the trade press and the local press in order to promote the park.

6. The park manager must be aware of the various advertising techniques and how they are used to promote his park. Examples are telephone book advertising, park brochures, post cards, park directories, signs, and posters.

7. The manager must be acquainted with the nature of manufacturer and dealer operations in the industry so that he may work with both dealers and manufacturers to assure that his park will be filled with residents at the earliest possible time. In this connection, he must be acquainted with environmental selling techniques.

8. Fundamental to a successful park operation is proper screening of new residents. The manager must be acquainted with the detailed steps and procedures for screening his prospective residents so as to provide a harmonious community.

9. The techniques which should be used in handling prospective residents so as to sell the desirable ones upon becoming a resident are of course extremely important.

10. The manager must know where to go to seek new residents and to what extent he is to be helpful in moving the resident in once he has decided to live

in the park.

11. A new manager must know proper techniques for becoming acquainted with tenants and for setting forth his policies. He must know how to handle those who resent a change in management.

12. A manager must know how to work with other park managers, dealers, and suppliers who service his park.

13. A manager must know the extent to which he can mix socially with his residents, how he should handle invitations from tenants, and how he should participate in social affairs in the park.

14. The manager must know how to handle tenants' suggestions and ideas and how he maintains a line of communication with residents. He must also be fully prepared to maintain control of the park without losing resident goodwill.

15. The manager must know how to handle specific trouble areas such as rent delinquencies, alcohol, noise, trouble makers, traffic violations, children, pets, maintenance complaints, etc.

Matters as listed above and a myriad of others must be handled by the park manager so as to assure a harmonious park. This is a difficult undertaking, possible only after orientation to the various techniques available to a park manager. Those managers who do not give attention to these details find themselves unpopular with their residents, a large number of vacancies, and a hostile community surrounding the park.

Public Relations

To a large extent the manager is a mayor of a small city; he is a politician and his public relations are extremely important to him. His public relations image spills over into all other facets of his activities. In promoting his park he is doing a public relations job. He must know how to assure both resident and community goodwill. He must know how to build a successful relationship between himself and the park owners. He must know how to favorably impress prospective residents. He must have a public relations program that relates to dealers, residents, manufacturers, suppliers, former residents, the press, the trades serving the park, other park communities, and the community itself. He must know how to participate in service clubs in the community, how to work with the chamber of commerce and in other community activities. He must know how to conduct a program which favorably impresses elected and appointed officials in the community, and he must know how to work with his local trade association. There are special techniques associated with each of these activities. The untrained or inexperienced manager may not only fail to know the techniques required but he may be oblivious to the fact that such activities are a necessary part of his job.

Insurance

A park manager has contact with insurance in several important ways. First of all, he should be qualified to advise as to the types of insurance that are required. Special types of insurance are frequently required in parks. Since the park's insurance is often to a large extent related to other insurance the owner carries, he must be aware of this relationship. The manager must know specifically what type of insurance the park requires so that he can be sure that it is properly covered to protect the investment of the owner. Furthermore, he should know how to shop for such insurance and how to obtain the most favorable rates consistent with an acceptable, qualified insurance carrier. The manager must be able to evaluate insurance costs as well as the service which is to be expected from the insurance company. The manager is often exposed to insurance adjustors, insurance inspectors, and to brokers who are seeking to obtain the park's insurance business. He must know how to deal with each. The manager must be fully aware of the relationship between negligence and insurance claims and keep this in mind in handling his maintenance functions.

Of critical importance to park harmony is the manager's knowledge of how to properly handle any insurance claims which may arise. He must know how to handle any claim which arises so as not to create disharmony in the park, but he must be equally aware of his responsibilities to the insurance carrier and not make unwarranted promises to residents concerning what the insurance company will or will not do. The manager must be aware of how to conduct himself in case of injury or accident so as not to violate the terms of the insurance contract. He should know what insurance policies are required in a park and which policies are unnecessary. He should be skilled in all techniques necessary to keep insurance costs at a minimum both from the point of view of what to buy as well as how to maintain his plant so as to eliminate unnecessary charges which may be assessed by an insurance company.

Legal Considerations

A park manager requires a considerable amount of legal knowledge in order to successfully operate his park. From a public relations point of view he must be knowledgeable in order to assure those with whom he has contact of his professionalism. He must have detailed knowledge of all legal matters which would be of interest to a resident insofar as it relates to their equipment. From a community point of view he must have a positive, constructive, forward looking approach to all legal matters. He should have a background of knowledge concerning mobile home law as well as recreational vehicle law. He needs knowledge on registration, taxes, fees, non-resident privileges, operator's license, brakes, safety device requirements, signal devices, tail lamps, reflectors, clearance, side marker lights, size limits, and permits for oversize vehicles. He needs to know how to select a knowledgeable and capable attorney to represent the park. His public relations image requires that he be able to refute unwarranted claims about the mobile home or recreational vehicle industry. The manager must understand the principles of zoning. He must understand his legal obligations relating to negligence, contracts into which the park may enter, registration of residents, and legal procedures for evictions. The manager must have detailed knowledge of all local legislation that affects the operation of his park. Further, he must know how to work with the legal authorities that have jurisdiction over his particular park.

Taxation

A substantial amount of the park's income is paid in taxes. The manager must be aware of the many types of taxes that affect his park as a necessary function of his financial management. He must understand property taxes and how to minimize them. He must understand his responsibility relating to licenses, fees, payroll taxes, sales taxes, and income taxes. Depreciation has a tremendous impact on park profits and the manager needs to understand depreciation and its relationship to park income so as to properly advise and counsel owners and CPA's who are working with him in connection with park operation. For public relations purposes the manager needs to be prepared to refute arguments to the effect that mobile homes or recreational vehicles do not pay their fair share of taxes in any given community.

Rules and Regulations

A successful manager must know how to present and administer a set of park rules and regulations which will assure tenant compliance and at the same time build tenant goodwill. Such rules will vary according to the location of the park and the type of the park. Residents must be persuaded to cooperate willingly and must understand why the rules are necessary. Rules cover such items as noise, condition of the mobile homes or recreational vehicle, condition of spaces and yards, the use of recreational facilities, payment of rent, gas, and electric bills, prohibiting the conduct of business, registration, use of telephones, law enforcement, use of public conveniences, parking, traffic control, refuse handling, group activity approval, peddling or soliciting, mail boxes, trespassing, visitors, curfews for children, television, etc. Such rules must be carefully written so as to assure compliance, and they must be published. The resident must sign, indicating that he has read and accepted the rules and regulations as set forth, and then they must be very carefully enforced so as to insure compliance. In this capacity the manager is acting as a policeman. This role is in conflict with his role as mayor. A very fine line must be walked; special techniques must be practiced.

Accounting

The park manager need not have extensive training in the field of accounting. All large parks have a CPA associated with them who handles the main part of the accounting work. The park manager does, however, need to understand how to read income statements and balance sheets since they are a reflection of the results of his operation of the park. He must be cost conscious and pay very careful attention to the operating statement. He must also have a minimum amount of budget training since any large park must of necessity operate on an annual budget.

The manager does require knowledge of bookkeeping systems as they are used in parks. The park office must bill residents monthly for rent, and may have to read power and gas meters and make the necessary billing computations. Individual record cards must be kept for each space reflecting the billing and income from that space. Receipts must be issued for payments made by residents, a cash receipts journal must be prepared, payments must be made for bills which the park incurs from its operation, and a cash payment journal must be prepared. Bank statements require reconciliation, and payroll must be prepared. Bank deposits must be prepared. In a large park all of these matters must be handled in the park office with the cash receipts journal and the cash payments journals forwarded to the park's CPA for entry into ledgers and preparation of financial statements. In connection with all of the office activity there are many forms. The manager must be trained to use each form.

Park Maintenance and Upkeep

Maintenance is a major responsibility for management. Lack of detailed park maintenance knowledge can lead to substantial and unnecessary expenses. The manager must know the details of maintenance; and he must know how to handle maintenance personnel. Maintenance requires daily inspection, knowledge of what to inspect, and knowledge of what action to take regarding all areas requiring attention. It is valuable for a manager to know approximately what percentage of the park's gross income should go to maintenance and housekeeping expenses. Work procedure charts must be prepared specifying what must be done, how often it is to be done, and what materials and tools are to be used. Mananagement must thoroughly understand maintenance of park plumbing, roads, grounds, buildings, and recreation facilities. Management must know how much maintenance personnel is required and what work standards can be expected from them. Management must know how to train and supervise maintenance personnel, how they should be uniformed, and how to instruct them concerning proper behavior in contact with both the public and residents so as to maintain a good public image for the park. A large number of forms are used in connection with maintenance to assure regularity and minimum costs. Good maintenance procedures require document files in the office, master maintenance records, and a maintenance calendar. Management must know what tools and supplies should be in the park maintenance room. Equally important is the manager's knowledge of health and safety hazards so that he will protect his residents and properly train his maintenance personnel to avoid hazards. Some park maintenance functions are less expensively handled by using outside services. The manager must know when to employ such services as contrasted with having the work done by regular park maintenance personnel. And last but certainly not least the manager must exercise very careful cost control in all his work.

Recreation and Social Activities

Management must understand the importance of tailoring park recreation programs to the desires of the residents. Such programs cannot be forced, of course. Management must understand the techniques that generate such programs if they are desired. If the park requires a social director, the manager must know the type of person to designate for this type of work and how to remunerate him. He must understand the duties to be delegated to the social director. Management must be familiar with the various outdoor activities, indoor activities, participant sports, and new trends in recreation as they apply to parks. Knowledge is required of equipment and rules and procedures for such activities as shuffleboard, archery, badminton, bicycling, bowling, croquet, golf, horseshoes, swimming and water sports, billiards, dancing, pot lucks, movies and slides, plays and skits, arts and crafts, sewing, ceramics, trips, library clubs, cards, checkers, ping pong, etc. Management must be aware of the cost connected with recreation and how and when to obtain the funds from the participants and when to have the park bear the cost. Scheduling procedures for recreation programs require careful attention. Management must know its part in recreation and the extent to which management itself should participate. Certain affairs should be sponsored by the park as a whole; in other cases the park is partially the sponsor. Holiday recreation activities are important in many parks; management must know its responsibilities in connection with them. Management must walk a very fine line in exercising control over tenant organizations and over recreation programs in which residents are involved. The techniques used to assure a harmonious recreation program are essential skills for management.

Park Personnel

As parks have become larger and larger the staff employed has enlarged. Management must know what personnel is required and understand the principles of park personnel management to assure efficient management and a relationship between residents and park personnel which would reflect a fine public relations image for the park. Management must know how to recruit, select, train, and motivate employees so as to be sure of efficiency. Management should know when to differentiate between adding employees and employing outside services. Efficient personnel management requires job descriptions, regular counseling, and supervision. Management must understand the techniques which must be used. As an assistant manager is an extremely important part of a large park, management must know the kind of person to employ and what rates of pay are fair.

Other Management Requirements

Efficient park operation requires a special relationship between ownership and the management of the park. This requires good communication between ownership and management and requires that management's authority must be clearly defined. Management must understand its obligations as well as the obligations of the owners. Management authority must be supported by the owners. Management must understand what reasonable salaries can be expected as remuneration and what types of management contracts are possible.

Establishing correct rental rates for a park is critical. There are serious pitfalls which must be avoided. Equally important is knowledge concerning when special inducements should or should not be used in filling a park.

Almost all parks earn a substantial amount of income from additional services other than payment of space rent. Management must understand how far it can properly go in seeking extra income. Management must have knowledge of how coin machines, laundry equipment, gas and electric meters provide extra income. There are many ethical considerations in providing extra income of which management must be aware. The difference between extra income potential of a mobile home park versus a recreational vehicle park must be understood. The relationship of the plant to extra income is important. Where the park is large, providing the opportunity to lease part of the park premises to outsiders for the conducting of business, knowledge is required concerning the proper relationship between these lessees, the amount of rent which can be realized and what types of businesses are acceptable. Management must also understand the extent to which it can get involved in the operation of such additional interest on park property.

Management Summary

This overview of the highlights of the responsibility of management emphasizes the complexity of the management responsibility and underlines our inability in a publication of this length to even begin to handle this subject in depth. Such material will be available in book form within the next several years. In the meantime, those who are interested in pursuing the subject of management in detail should contact Park Management Associates, Box 1417, Beverly Hills, California 90213. This firm markets a home study course which trains management for the industry. The course may be purchased outright for reference purposes.

How To Obtain Park Management

At the present, there is a scarcity of personnel with experience, training, and knowledge in the field of park management. This scarcity must continue for a considerable period of time. The industry is expanding rapidly, proper training of personnel is time consuming, and the new developer may find himself with a difficult problem in obtaining the required qualified management.

There are a large number of newspapers which circulate in mobile home and recreational vehicle parks among its residents. A list of such publications can be obtained from the Mobile Homes Manufacturers association, whose address is given in the introduction to this publication. Placing an ad for management personnel in the correct regional publication will bring many responses from those who want to undertake such a career or who are already involved in the industry and are seeking a change.

Park Management Associates, whose address is given immediately above, operates a placement service for its graduates. Inquiries can be made to it concerning management needs. Qualified individuals are referred to ownership.

Professional Property Management

Another approach to management which may be desirable (especially for ownership which does not want to be concerned with day to day details of operating a park) is to rely upon professional property management. Park Management Associates offer such a service and will send you details upon receipt of your request for information. There are other firms located throughout the United States which offer such services, and they can be located by contacting industry trade associations.

Park management under property management contract usually involves a fee somewhere in the vicinity of 5 percent of gross receipts; this fee may often be negotiated to a slightly lesser percentage if the property to be managed is large, with a substantial income flow. Even though property management can involve a substantial fee to the firm handling that management, a well qualified firm will more than earn its fee through its expertise in the industry. Through "know-how" such firms minimize expenses and maximize revenues.

APPENDIX

APPENDIX

To demonstrate the comprehensiveness of the investigative procedure required for proper investment analysis of a proposed park we are printing in this appendix excerpts from a feasibility study prepared by Park Management Associates. The park name has of course been changed. The complete study covered about 150 pages; we are reproducing only a few pages here.

A preliminary interview with the client revealed that a feasibility study would probably result in a favorable recommendation for a park on the proposed 55 acres, so an experienced field man was flown to the city in which the land was located. The use of *experienced and trained* personnel for a field study of local conditions is, of course, a requirement. Whoever conducts such a survey must know what questions to ask, how to ask them, and how to evaluate the answers to obtain the *real* facts. The actual field work required five days.

First the property was visited. Area maps, topo maps and aerial photos were obtained. Interviews were conducted with trade associations, the planning commission, Chamber of Commerce, every mobile home dealer and every park in the community, real estate brokers, local financial institutions, County Flood Control Board, contractors, architects, building department, tax assessor, licensing agencies, and all utility companies including sewage district, gas, power, water, trash collection, telephone, and TV antenna companies.

Each interview was summarized comprehensively on a questionnaire. Some of the questionnaires require as many as six pages for a single interview. The field man also shot numerous pictures of competitive parks and their facilities, the facilities of dealerships, and photos of the land itself.

An analysis of the collected data revealed the following facts:

1. Although there were many parks already in the community, all but a few were of poor quality.
2. All parks in the area worthy of consideration by a prospective resident were full.
3. There was strong demand for spaces, yet no new parks were under construction, nor had there been zoning requests for new parks. The one exception was a new park that had been open a month and was filling rapidly.
4. The time required to fill a new quality park of 300 spaces, having both a family section and an all adult section, appeared to be about one year.
5. Competition was such that a monthly rental of $47.50 would rapidly attract residents.
6. The community would look with favor on a deluxe mobile home park.
7. Zoning was easily obtainable.
8. The land was favorably located with respect to transportation, shopping, schools, and churches.
9. All utilities were available at the property line except sewers and water. The soil was suitable for a septic system and sufficient land was available for such a sewage system. Adequate water was available from wells already on the property. There were no flood control problems.
10. The location was free of negative factors which might make residential living undesirable at that location.
11. Soil conditions were suitable for park construction.

Because the survey indicated the community needed a new park and that the proposed 55 acre land was a suitable site, an experienced park architect was flown there. He prepared a plot plan for the park and a cost projection. He also prepared preliminary plans for park buildings.

Although there was enough land to build a 440 space park, it was decided to develop the land in two phases because:

1. A combination park was to be built having a family section and an all-adult section. By placing the adult section at one end of the property and the family section at the other, the section in the center could be later developed as either a family or adult section, or both, depending on demand for spaces.
2. Initial investment could be held within the capabilities of the park owners; future expansion could be financed by park earnings.

The architect therefore prepared separate cost projections for Phase I and Phase II of the development.

The pages which follow have been taken from the completed study and show:

1. Park feautres (pages A, B)
2. Cost of construction for Phases I and II (pages C, D).
3. Summary of investment analysis data (page E). This sheet reveals project cost to be $753,000, investors cash requirements to be $89,424 and a cash flow from Phase I of about 20 percent on invested capital. In this study, at the client's request, no cost was included for loan points or contingencies. These costs would show in a normal projected investment analysis.
4. A pro forma operating statement for three years with footnotes to substantiate computations. (Pages F, G, H, I, J). Note that circumstances pertaining to that particular location are used in projections rather than so called industry averages. Note, too, that even though anticipated filling rate is one year, a two year filling rate is used for financial projections. This is to provide a safety factor. A two year basis for filling (with a 5 percent vacancy factor) is favored by loan companies in projections for loan commitments.
5. Rate at which loan will pay off (page K).
6. Rate of return (page L). Note that actual return is a combination of cash flow (N/S) and equity build-

up. The right hand column shows total return percentage on investment.

7. Depreciation allowances (page M).
8. Income tax analysis (page N). Note that by using loss carry back provisions of the tax law, income is sheltered for over six years. The first two years of operations show losses. Later, profits may be carried back against these losses to provide a zero income for tax purposes. Thus, even though the investor is receiving $61,666 a year (see page E), no income tax is paid on it.

Additional facts must be considered to realize the true investment potential of this particular project.

1. Land values in this area were shown to be appreciating at 8 percent each year.
2. Within five years rental rates might realistically rise to $65.00 if excellent management is retained.
3. The park will probably fill in one year reducing cash needs for loan payment in first and second year.
4. Land is owned and paid for which will permit a 172 space expansion for a cost of only $1,368.00 per space. A full financial projection for the 440 space park would show a much higher return on investment than is shown for the Phase I development only.

APPENDIX

QRS MOBILE HOME PARK

PARK FEATURES

o One Hundred Fifty-six (156) Spaces for Adults

o One Hundred Twelve (112) Spaces for Families

o One Hundred Seventy-two (172) Spaces can be Built at a Later Date in Area Separating Adult and Family Park.

o Adult Area Recreation Center Includes:

    ° Visitor Parking

    ° Casting Pool

    ° Horseshoes

    ° Two (2) Shuffleboard Courts

    ° Putting Green

    ° Laundry With Drying Yard

    ° Swimming Pool

o Recreation Building With:

    ° Rest Rooms

    ° Kitchen

    ° Office

    ° Large Recreation Room

    ° Card Room

    ° Billiard Room

    ° Library

o Family Area Recreation Center Includes:

    ° Skating Rink

    ° Sand Pit

    ° Basketball Court

    ° Jungle Jim

A

- ° Tether Ball
- ° Volley Ball Court
- ° Hand Ball Court
- ° Visitor Parking
- ° Drying Yard and Laundry
- ° Swimming Pool
- o Recreation Building With:
  - ° Library
  - ° Office
  - ° Snack Bar
  - ° Rest Rooms
- o Underground Utilities
- o Asphalt Streets
- o Asphalt Guest Parking Areas
- o Car Wash Area
- o Fenced Drying and Trash Areas
- o Individually Metered Power
- o Fencing and Block Wall
- o Two Car Parking on Each Lot

QRS MOBILE HOME PARK

PHASE I

156 Adult Spaces
112 Family Spaces

ESTIMATED ONSITE COSTS

Plans, specifications, and engineering	$ 20,000.00
Plan check and permits	--
Engineering, site -- staking	5,300.00
Excavating - Grading - Clearing	7,300.00
Fine grading	3,900.00
Concrete	10,600.00
Plumbing, water, gas, sewer distribution	134,000.00
Gas operated water system with well, pump and storage tank	22,500.00
Electrical power distribution	76,000.00
Telephone	--
Fencing, masonry	2,500.00
Wood	500.00
Wire	7,750.00
Asphaltic concrete paving for streets, parking, and visitor parking	68,000.00
Recreation Buildings	85,000.00
Gravel for under mobile home	8,040.00
Swimming pools	8,000.00
Miscellaneous signs	700.00
Painting	1,300.00
Clothes lines	600.00
Mailboxes	2,150.00
Coll. stations	2,400.00
Parking bumpers and striping	500.00
Landscaping	6,500.00
Clean-up	1,000.00
Temporary facilities water Office - Tel. - Elec.	800.00
Supervision	4,500.00
Insurance	700.00

1st Phase - Total Cost	$ 480,500.00
Oh and profit	53,000.00
Total	$ 533,500.00
Cost per Site	$ 1,991.00

QRS MOBILE HOME PARK

PHASE II

These Costs Not Considered In Present Projections For 268 Space Park

172 Adult or Family Spaces as Possible Future Expansion

ESTIMATED ONSITE COST

Plans, specifications, and engineering	$ --
Plan check and permits	--
Engineering, site -- staking	3,400.00
Excavating - Grading - Clearing	4,500.00
Fine Grading	2,500.00
Concrete	3,300.00
Plumbing, water, gas, sewer distribution	86,000.00
Gas operated water system with well, pump and	
storage tank	15,500.00
Electrical power distribution	45,000.00
Telephone	--
Fencing, masonry	--
Wood	--
Wire	--
Asphaltic concrete paving for streets, lot	
parking, visitor parking	34,150.00
Recreation buildings	--
Gravel for under mobile home	5,160.00
Swimming pools	--
Miscellaneous signs	200.00
Painting	300.00
Clothes lines	--
Mailboxes	1,400.00
Coll. stations	1,400.00
Parking bumpers and striping	100.00
Landscaping	5,000.00
Clean-up	400.00
Temporary facilities water	--
Office - Tel. - Elec.	700.00
Supervision	2,600.00
Insurance	600.00
2nd Phase - Total Cost	$212,210.00
Oh and Profit	23,000.00
Total	$235,210.00
Cost per Site	$ 1,368.00

APPENDIX

PROJECTED INVESTMENT IN

QRS MOBILE HOME PARK

Land 55 Acres @ $4,000 per Acre.........$220,000
Construction Costs.................... 533,500

    Total Cost. . . . . $ 753,500

Anticipated First Trust Deed (75 percent
 of value of land plus construction)
 10 percent Loan For 20 Years...........$565,000
Investor's Capital Needs:
  Excess of Cost over Mortgage Loan..... 188,500
  Construction Loan Interest........... 35,000
  Working Capital...................... 25,000

Loan Payment 1st Year:
    Amount Due $65,427.00
    1st Year Cash Available   4,503.00 60,924

Loan Payment 2nd Year:
    Amount Due $65,427.00
    2nd Year Cash Available 79,052.00 -o-

   Total Investor Capital Required   309,424
   Less Land Value   220,000

   Required Cash Investment $ 89,424

Computation of Investment Return

Estimated Income (after 2 years)   174,917
Estimated Annual Expense   47,824
Estimated Net Before Debt Service   127,093

Payment on $565,000 1st Trust Deed
 for 20 years @ 10 percent interest   65,427

   Estimated Net To Investor   61,666

Spendable Return on Cash and Land Investment
           of $309,324.00 =   19.94%

Plus Equity Gain On 1st Trust Deed (See Schedules)

E

APPENDIX

QRS MOBILE HOME PARK

ESTIMATED OPERATING INCOME, COSTS AND NET

FIRST THREE YEARS OF OPERATION

ESTIMATED INCOME	FIRST YEAR MONTHLY	YEARLY
Space Rents (1)	$ 3,135.00	
Extra Occupancy (2)	152.75	
GROSS RENT INCOME	$ 3,287.75	
OTHER INCOME		
Utility Sales (3)	$ 66.00	
Vending Machine Income (4)	19.80	
Washing Machine Income (5)	66.00	
TOTAL ESTIMATED INCOME	$ 3,439.55	$ 41,274.60
ESTIMATED OPERATING EXPENSES:		
Property Taxes (6)	$ 384.28	
Salaries (7)	1,050.00	
Water (8)	50.00	
Insurance (9)	60.00	
Office Expense	75.00	
Advertising (10)	290.00	
Telephone	50.00	
Utilities	400.00	
Laundry Expense	50.00	
Maintenance (11)	300.00	
Legal and Professional	100.00	
Business Fees and Licenses (12)	25.00	
Trash Pick-Up (13)	120.00	
Entertainment (14)	20.00	
Dues and Subscriptions	40.00	
Miscellaneous	50.00	
TOTAL ESTIMATED EXPENSES	$ 3,064.28	$ 36,771.36

NET ESTIMATED INCOME BEFORE
DEPRECIATION, INTEREST AND
INCOME TAXES $ 4,503.24

F

SECOND YEAR		THIRD YEAR	
MONTHLY	YEARLY	MONTHLY	YEARLY
$9,191.25		$13,323.75	
459.56		666.19	
$9,650.81		$13,989.94	
$ 193.30		$ 255.00	
58.05		76.50	
193.50		255.00	
10,095.66	$121,147.92	$14,576.44	$ 174,917.28
$ 423.01		$ 465.31	
1,150.00		1,150.00	
50.00		125.00	
60.00		60.00	
85.00		95.00	
205.00		75.00	
50.00		50.00	
500.00		700.00	
50.00		50.00	
500.00		700.00	
100.00		100.00	
25.00		25.00	
180.00		240.00	
30.00		40.00	
50.00		60.00	
50.00		50.00	
$3,508.01	42,096.12	$ 3,985.31	$ 47,823.72
	$ 79,051.80		$ 127,093.56

G

APPENDIX

<u>FOOTNOTES ON QRS MOBILE HOME PARK INCOME STATEMENT</u>

(1) Assume spaces will rent in proportion to availability and that there will be a linear increase in occupancy.

There are: 268 spaces @ $47.50 per month

<u>FIRST YEAR</u>

Assume park is 50 percent full at end of first year. Gross revenue for year is:

$$132 \text{ spaces x } \$47.50 \div 2 = \$3,135.00 \text{ per month}$$

<u>SECOND YEAR</u>

Assume park is 95 percent full at end of second year. Gross revenue for year is:

$$(132 \text{ spaces x } \$47.50) + (123 \text{ spaces x } \$47.50 \div 2) = \$9,191.25$$
per month.

<u>THIRD YEAR</u>

Assume 95 percent occupancy and a 10 percent rent increase. Gross revenue for year is:

$$255 \text{ spaces x } \$47.50 \text{ x } \$1.10 = \$13,323.75 \text{ per month}$$

(2) **Extra** Occupancy Rates Should Be:

Pets $2.00 per month, guests $5.00 per month, more than 2 persons per mobile home $1.00 per person. Should generate 5 percent increase in rents.

(3) Power will be metered by power company. No profit to park. Park will set a monthly rate for gas which will bring park a profit of $1.00 per occupied space.

Making same assumptions as in note (1) above computations are:

<u>FIRST YEAR</u>

$$132 \text{ spaces x } \$1.00 \div 2 = \$66.00 \text{ per month}$$

<u>SECOND YEAR</u>

$$(132 \text{ spaces x } \$1.00) + (123 \text{ spaces x } \$1.00 \div 2) = \$193.50$$
per month

H

<u>THIRD YEAR</u>

Assume no increase in these charges.

255 spaces x $1.00 = $255.00 per month

(4) Make same assumptions as in note (1) above. Based on
earning 30¢ per space per month.

<u>FIRST YEAR</u>

132 spaces x $.30 ÷ 2 = $19.80 per month

<u>SECOND YEAR</u>

(132 spaces x $.30) + (123 spaces x $.30 ÷ 2) = $58.05

<u>THIRD YEAR</u>

255 spaces x $.30 = $76.50 per month

(5) Make same assumptions as in note (1) above.
Based on park profit of $1.00 per occupied space per month.

<u>FIRST YEAR</u>

132 spaces x $1.00 ÷2= $66.00 per month

<u>SECOND YEAR</u>

(132 spaces x $1.00) + (123 spaces x $1.00 ÷ 2) = $193.50
                                                          per month

<u>THIRD YEAR</u>

255 spaces x $1.00 = $255.00 per month

(6) Present full value of land is 55 acres x $4,000 per
acre = $220,000
Construction cost Phase 1 is: 533,500
Tax Base is: $753,500

For tax purpose 20 percent of value is
assessed valuation

                Assessed Valuation = $150,700

Tax rate is $3.06 per $100.00 of appraised value (state
47¢, county 95¢, school district $1.64).

Monthly property taxes are:

    $1,507.00 x $3.06 ÷ 12 = $384.28

We have assumed taxes will increase 10 percent per year.

I

(7) Manager and wife $750.00 per month plus space and
     utilities
     Assistant manager and wife $400.00 per month plus
     space and utilities. First year needed 9 months only.

FIRST YEAR

   ($750.00 x 12) + ($400.00 x 9) ÷ 12 = $1,050.00 per month

SUBSEQUENT YEARS

      $ 750.00
        400.00
      $1150.00 per month

(8) Park has well, pump, and storage tank maintenance cost
    first and second year $50 per month. Thereafter $120
    per month.

(9) Covers compensation, fire, and extended coverage on
    park property, liability, and medical coverage.

(10) The cost of advertising literature is amortized over
     the first year. The cost of newspaper and magazine
     advertising is shown for two years thereafter adver-
     tising is limited to telephone directory and industry
     directory listings.

	First Year	Second Year COST PER MONTH	Third Year
Advertising literature	$125.00	$ 40.00	$ 10.00
Media Advertising	100.00	100.00	---
Directories	65.00	65.00	65.00
TOTALS	$290.00	$205.00	$ 75.00

(11) Because plant is new cost is less in early years. In a
     normal park it averages 5 percent of gross receipts.

(12) To cover possible annual license fees.

(13) Eight three-cubic-yard containers requred with pick
     up twice a week. Rate quoted is:

     8 x $30.00 = $240.00

     Fewer containers necessary when park is not full.

(14) Covers park's share of costs in entertaining park
     tenants.

J

QRS MOBILE HOME PARK

LOAN AMORTIZATION TABLE

YEAR	INTEREST	PRINCIPAL	TOTAL PAYMENT	BALANCE
0				$565,000.00
1	$56,077.00	$ 9,350.00	$65,427.00	555,650.00
2	55,099.00	10,328.00	65,427.00	545,322.00
3	54,018.00	11,409.00	65,427.00	533,913.00
4	52,822.00	12,605.00	65,427.00	521,308.00
5	51,503.00	13,924.00	65,427.00	507,384.00
6	50,044.00	15,383.00	65,427.00	492,001.00
7	48,434.00	16,993.00	65,427.00	475,008.00
8	46,655.00	18,772.00	65,427.00	456,236.00
9	44,688.00	20,739.00	65,427.00	435,497.00
10	42,517.00	22,910.00	65,427.00	412,587.00
11	40,120.00	25,307.00	65,427.00	387,278.00
12	37,468.00	27,959.00	65,427.00	359,319.00
13	34,541.00	30,886.00	65,427.00	328,433.00
14	31,306.00	34,121.00	65,427.00	294,312.00
15	27,733.00	37,694.00	65,427.00	256,618.00
16	23,786.00	41,641.00	65,427.00	214,977.00
17	19,426.00	46,001.00	65,427.00	168,976.00
18	14,609.00	50,818.00	65,427.00	118,158.00
19	9,287.00	56,140.00	65,427.00	62,018.00
20	3,409.00	62,018.00	65,427.00	-0-

APPENDIX

QRS MOBILE HOME PARK

DOUBLE DECLINING BALANCE DEPRECIATION SCHEDULE

BASED ON 17-YEAR USEFUL LIFE

YEAR	DEPRECIATION	BOOK VALUE
0	-0-	$533,500.00
1	$ 62,764.00	470,736.00
2	55,380.00	415,356.00
3	48,864.00	366,492.00
4	43,116.00	323,376.00
5	38,044.00	285,332.00
6	33,568.00	251,764.00
7	29,618.00	222,146.00
8	26,134.00	196,012.00
9	23,060.00	172,952.00
10	20,346.00	152,606.00
11	17,952.00	134,654.00
12	15,840.00	118,814.00
13	13,978.00	104,836.00
14	12,332.00	92,504.00
15	10,882.00	81,622.00
16	9,602.00	72,020.00
17	8,472.00	63,548.00

L

QRS MOBILE HOME PARK

RETURN ON NET SPENDABLE AND EQUITY BUILD UP

VERSUS INVESTMENT OF $309,324.00

YEAR	NET SPENDABLE	% RETURN ON N/S	EQUITY BUILD UP ON FIRST TRUST DEED	% RETURN ON E/B	TOTAL N/S + E/B	% RETURN ON N/S + E/B
1	$ -0-		$ 9,350.00	3.02%	$ 9,350.00	3.02%
2	13,625.00	4.40%	10,328.00	3.34%	23,953.00	7.74%
3	61,666.00	19.94%	11,409.00	3.69%	73,075.00	23.63%
4	61,666.00	19.94%	12,605.00	4.08%	74,271.00	24.02%
5	61,666.00	19.94%	13,924.00	4.50%	75,590.00	24.44%
6	61,666.00	19.94%	15,383.00	4.97%	77,049.00	24.91%
7	61,666.00	19.94%	16,993.00	5.49%	78,659.00	25.43%
8	61,666.00	19.94%	18,772.00	6.07%	80,438.00	26.01%
9	61,666.00	19.94%	20,739.00	6.70%	82,405.00	26.64%
10	61,666.00	19.94%	22,910.00	7.41%	84,576.00	27.35%
11	61,666.00	19.94%	'25,307.00	8.18%	86,973.00	28.12%
12	61,666.00	19.94%	27,959.00	9.04%	89,625.00	28.98%
13	61,666.00	19.94%	30,886.00	9.99%	92,552.00	29.93%
14	61,666.00	19.94%	34,121.00	11.03%	95,787.00	30.97%
15	61,666.00	19.94%	37,694.00	12.19%	99,360.00	32.13%
16	61,666.00	19.94%	41,641.00	13.46%	103,307.00	33.40%
17	61,666.00	19.94%	46,001.00	14.87%	107,667.00	34.81%
18	61,666.00	19.94%	50,818.00	16.43%	112,484.00	36.37%
19	61,666.00	19.94%	56,140.00	18.15%	117,806.00	38.09%
20	61,666.00	19.94%	62,018.00	20.05%	123,684.00	39.99%
21 and after	127,093.00	39.88	-0-	-0-	127,093.00	39.99%

QRS MOBILE HOME PARK

TAXABLE INCOME ANALYSIS

YEAR	OPERATING INCOME	LESS DEPRECIATION	LESS INTEREST	NET TAXABLE INCOME
1	[$ 4,503.00]	$ 62,764.00	$56,077.00	[$114,338.00]
2	79,052.00	55,380.00	55,099.00	[31,427.00]
3	127,094.00	48,864.00	54,018.00	24,212.00
4	127,094.00	43,116.00	52,822.00	31,156.00
5	127,094.00	38,044.00	51,503.00	37,547.00
6	127,094.00	33,568.00	50,044.00	43,482.00
7	127,094.00	29,618.00	48,434.00	49,042.00
8	127,094.00	26,134.00	46,655.00	54,305.00
9	127,094.00	23,060.00	44,688.00	59,346.00
10	127,094.00	20,346.00	42,517.00	64,231.00
11	127,094.00	17,952.00	40,120.00	69,022.00
12	127,094.00	15,840.00	37,468.00	73,786.00
13	127,094.00	13,978.00	34,541.00	78,575.00
14	127,094.00	12,332.00	31,306.00	83,456.00
15	127,094.00	10,882.00	27,733.00	88,539.00
16	127,094.00	9,602.00	23,786.00	93,706.00
17	127,094.00	8,472.00	19,426.00	99,196.00
18	127,094.00	-0-	14,609.00	112,485.00
19	127,094.00	-0-	9,287.00	117,807.00
20	127,094.00	-0-	3,409.00	123,685.00
21	127,094.00	-0-	-0-	127,094.00